CHARACTERS

A one-year exploration of the Bible
through the lives of its people.

VOLUME THREE

The Kings

LifeWay Press® • Nashville, Tennessee

EDITORIAL TEAM

Brandon Hiltibidal
Director, Discipleship and Groups Ministry

Brian Daniel
Manager, Short-Term Discipleship

Joel Polk
Editorial Team Leader

Ken Braddy
Content Developer

David Briscoe
Content Developer

G.B. Howell Jr.
Content Developer

Rob Tims
Content Editor

Laura Magness
Content Editor

Gena Rogers
Production Editor

Darin Clark
Art Director

Denise Wells
Designer

Lauren Rives
Designer

From the creators of *Explore the Bible, Explore the Bible: Characters* is a seven-volume resource that examines the lives of biblical characters within the historical, cultural, and biblical context of Scripture. Each six-session volume includes videos to help your group understand the way each character fits into the storyline of the Bible.

© 2020 LifeWay Press®

ISBN 978-1-4300-7037-5 • Item 005823505
Dewey decimal classification: 220.92
Subject headings: BIBLE. O.T.--BIOGRAPHY / KINGS, BIBLICAL

We believe that the Bible has God for its author; salvation for its end; and truth, without any mixture of error, for its matter and that all Scripture is totally true and trustworthy. To review LifeWay's doctrinal guideline, please visit lifeway.com/doctrinalguideline.

Scripture quotations are taken from the Christian Standard Bible®, Copyright © 2017 by Holman Bible Publishers. Used by permission. Christian Standard Bible® and CSB® are federally registered trademarks of Holman Bible Publishers.

To order additional copies of this resource, write to LifeWay Resources Customer Service; One LifeWay Plaza; Nashville, TN 37234; fax 615-251-5933; call toll free 800-458-2772; or order online at LifeWay.com; email orderentry@lifeway.com.

Printed in the United States of America

Groups Ministry Publishing • LifeWay Resources
One LifeWay Plaza • Nashville, TN 37234

CONTENTS

ABOUT EXPLORE THE BIBLE

The Whole Truth, Book by Book

Explore the Bible is an ongoing family of Bible study resources that guides the whole church through the only source of the truth on which we can rely: God's Word. Each session frames Scripture with biblical and historical context vital to understanding its original intent, and unpacks the transforming truth of God's Word in a manner that is practical, age-appropriate, and repeatable over a lifetime.

To find out more, at goExploreTheBible.com.

HOW TO USE THIS STUDY

This Bible-study book includes six sessions of content for group and personal study. Regardless of what day of the week your group meets, each session begins with group study. Each group session utilizes the following elements to facilitate simple yet meaningful interaction among group members and with God's Word.

INTRODUCTION

This page includes introductory content and questions to get the conversation started each time your group meets.

GROUP DISCUSSION

Each session has a corresponding teaching video to help tell the story. These videos have been created specifically to teach the group more about the biblical figure being studied. After watching the video, continue the group discussion by reading the Scripture passages and discussing the questions on these pages. Finally, conclude each group session with a time of prayer, reflecting on what you have discussed.

BIOGRAPHY AND FURTHER INSIGHT MOMENT

These sections provide more in-depth information regarding the biblical character being spotlighted each week and can be included in the group discussion or personal study times.

PERSONAL STUDY

Three personal studies are provided for each session to take individuals deeper into Scripture and to supplement the content introduced in the group study. With biblical teaching and introspective questions, these sections challenge individuals to grow in their understanding of God's Word and to respond in faith.

LEADER GUIDE

A tear-out leader guide for each session is provided on pages 95-106. This section also includes sample answers or discussion prompts to help you jump-start or steer the conversation.

VOLUME THREE

The Kings

SAUL

Israel's First King

INTRODUCTION

Why do we often believe we know a better way than God's way?

The people of Israel had come a long way since the days of slavery in Egypt. One of their most revered leaders, Moses, had been appointed by God to bring His people into the promised land. Once there, each of Israel's twelve tribes was given sections of the land to occupy, and the people began life in their new home.

As the people of God grew in number, they became a nation. When the people of God compared themselves to other nations, they realized a major difference: God's people had no earthly king to rule them, so they cried out for one. This was a rejection of their heavenly King who had freed them from slavery and provided for them in the exodus from Egypt.

God allowed the people to have what they wanted, and through the prophet Samuel, an earthly king was chosen. Saul, Israel's first king, would not prove to be a perfect king. Because Saul disobeyed God's command during a specific crisis, God rejected him as king. Obedience to God, even when we think we have a better way, is always best. King Saul learned a very difficult lesson about the price of disobedience.

When you were younger, what rules did you have to follow in your home that felt unnecessary?

Why is it important to obey God, even in the little things we might think are not important?

Watch the video teaching for Session 1 to discover "The World of King Saul," then continue the group discussion.

GROUP DISCUSSION

FOCUS ATTENTION

How might adding ingredients to or deleting ingredients from a recipe have disastrous results? What are the benefits of following a recipe to the letter?

EXPLORE THE TEXT

As a group, read 1 Samuel 13:1,5-14.

In what ways did Saul disobey God in these verses, and why was his disobedience so serious? In what ways can fear prompt people to disobey God?

Do you feel that Saul's punishment was suitable to the consequences he suffered? Why or why not?

As a group, read 1 Samuel 15:1-3.

Why did the Amalekites deserve such a severe punishment? What does this show you about God's character?

As a group, read 1 Samuel 15:7-15,20-23.

Yet again, Saul and his army only partially complied with the Lord's command. Why did they disobey this time? What was the Lord's reaction to this?

Saul built a monument to himself. Based on this, what did he think about himself, and what did he think about God?

Do you think Saul was truly surprised that his behaviors were sinful, or do you think he was attempting to redefine his disobedience as something acceptable? Explain.

APPLY THE TEXT

To obey means to hear God and act accordingly. Several words for obedience in both the Old and New Testaments associate hearing and doing God's will. Another New Testament word for obedience means trust. A person who trusts God does what He says. Why? Gratitude for God's grace causes us to love God and want to do His will. As we obey God, we experience the blessings He longs to share with us; on the other hand, disobedience produces judgment and necessary discipline. As we obey, we acknowledge the priority of God's mission over our own concerns.

Why is partial obedience to God, even substantial obedience, insufficient?

In what ways can our group encourage one another to obey God more fully in all areas of faith and life?

"To obey is better than sacrifice" (1 Sam. 15:22). In what areas are you substituting sacrifice for obedience?

Close your group time in prayer, reflecting on what you have discussed.

SAUL

KEY VERSES

Samuel said to Saul, "You have been foolish. You have not kept the command the LORD your God gave you. It was at this time that the LORD would have permanently established your reign over Israel, but now your reign will not endure."

— 1 Samuel 13:13-14a

BASIC FACTS

1. Son of Kish, of the tribe of Benjamin, who became the first king of Israel.

2. Name *Saul* means "asked for."

3. Anointed as king by Samuel the prophet; publicly elected by a process of casting lots.

4. Was thirty years old when he became king; ruled Israel for forty-two years.

5. Married to Ahinoam [uh HIN oh am]; had six children, including Jonathan and Michal.

6. Died in battle against Philistines; wounded by enemy arrows, then fell on his sword.

TIMELINE

1200–1100 BC

- "Sea Peoples" invade western Canaan 1200
- Jephthah 1200–1150
- Gideon defeats Midianites-Amalekites 1200
- Ruth 1175–1125
- Jephthah defeats Ammonites-Philistines 1170
- Samson 1120–1060

1100–1050 BC

- Samuel 1105–1025
- Saul 1080–1010
- Death of Eli, priest at Shiloh 1070
- Twenty-first Dynasty in Egypt 1069–945
- Samson defeats enemies in death at Gaza 1060

KNOWN FOR

1. Saul was physically impressive, standing a head taller than most Israelites (1 Sam. 9:2).

2. He was a valiant soldier, yet a paranoid and impulsive commander (1 Sam. 13:3-4,10-12).

3. He delivered the people of Jabesh-gilead from humiliation by Ammonites (1 Sam. 11:1-11).

4. He reigned as Israel's king for forty-two years, yet in the end failed because he disobeyed God (1 Sam. 15:17-29).

5. Saul took David into his royal administration but later made several attempts on David's life in fits of jealous rage (1 Sam. 18–21).

6. Saul killed eighty-five priests and wiped out the priestly town of Nob because he suspected the priests of conspiring with David (1 Sam. 22:11-19).

7. Saul visited the witch of En-dor in an effort to contact the dead prophet Samuel for guidance (1 Sam. 28).

8. In a battle against the Philistines, Saul's three sons were killed and the king was severely wounded. To avoid capture and torture, Saul fell on his own sword and died. The Philistines beheaded the king's body and hung it on the wall of Beth-shan. The people of Jabesh-gilead later retrieved Saul's body, cremated it, and buried the king's bones under a tree in their town (1 Sam. 31).

1050–1000 BC	1000–950 BC
Saul chosen as first king of Israel 1050	Chinese store ice for refrigeration 1000
David 1040–970	David conquers Jerusalem; moves ark 1000
David becomes king of Judah 1010	Absalom revolts against David 975
David becomes king of all Israel 1003	Solomon 990–931
	David dies; Solomon anointed king 970
	Temple of Solomon completed 959

Saul, Israel's Failed King

By Eric A. Mitchell

When Samuel was old, the elders and people of Israel demanded a king (see 1 Sam. 8). God described this demand as rebellion against Him (see 8:7-9). But God allowed this king as a test—giving the people His warning that the king would oppress them, take their goods, and enslave them (see 8:10-18). God gave them Saul.

Saul possessed good looks and was taller than any other Israelite (see 9:2). When Goliath defied Israel and demanded an Israelite warrior to fight, Saul should have stepped forward. He had been appointed king for this very reason (see 8:20). Instead, Saul and all Israel were fearful, and Saul did not go out for forty consecutive days (see 17:10-11,16).

Saul was not a competent leader. As Saul looked for the donkeys, his servant was the one who encouraged him to seek Samuel's advice (see ch. 9). His servant carried the money to pay Samuel for his services. Young girls in Ramah pointed and gave Saul directions to find Samuel. Saul's hometown of Gibeah was only a few miles from Samuel's town of Ramah, and yet Saul seemingly knew nothing of Samuel, Israel's long-serving spiritual leader and judge.

Saul missed out on his commission. Samuel had commissioned Saul to go to "Gibeah of God where there are Philistine garrisons" (10:5) and "do whatever your circumstances require because God is with you" (10:7). Saul was then to go to Gilgal and wait for Samuel seven days until he (Samuel) came to offer sacrifices and tell Saul what to do next (see 10:8). But despite the signs from God and the Spirit of God coming upon him, Saul did none of the things Samuel had instructed.

When Samuel gathered Israel at Mizpah and cast lots to choose the king from among the people, Saul was fearfully hiding among the baggage (see 10:17-22). Afterward, Saul went home to farm, again ignoring Samuel's commission (see 11:4). When the

Eric A. Mitchell, "Saul, Israel's Failed King," *Biblical Illustrator*, Summer 2019.

Ammonites attacked Israel (see 11:1-3), Saul did not ask Israel to follow him into battle; instead he threatened them if they did not (see 11:6-7). After Saul delivered Israel from the Ammonites, God judged the land by sending a crop-destroying thunderstorm during the dry season, because the people rejected His rule and failed His test by choosing a king over Him (see 12:12-25).

The Book of 1 Samuel highlights Saul's disobedience, missed opportunities, lack of integrity, sordid actions, and foolish words. Saul was given the opportunity for both kingship and a dynasty, but he never met the standards for kingship in Deuteronomy 17:14-20. Further, he did not fulfill his commission, and to the end was disobedient to God's commands (see 1 Sam. 15:3,9). All of this led to God's rejecting Saul and selecting David as Israel's next king.

After being anointed as king, Saul returned to his hometown of Gibeah where he later built his royal palace.

Read 1 Samuel 13:6-14.

It is God's expectation that His holy character be reflected in the lives of His people through obedience to His commands. King Saul chose to disobey God when he allowed his soldiers to take plunder from their battle with the Amalekites, and he also disobeyed when he spared the Amalekite king's life. Partial obedience is still disobedience.

What excuses do believers make to justify disobeying God? To partially obeying His commands?

At many points in our lives, we adhere to a form of situational ethics whereby we act based on what "feels right," "seems right," or what "everyone else is doing." We may desire to please God, but struggle to obey Him. We have the most difficulty when obedience puts us at a disadvantage or even in danger. Yet God expects His people to obey Him boldly and completely.

Saul, Israel's first king, had every advantage. Samuel, the prophet, was there to anoint him king and to guide him in spiritual matters. Saul's son Jonathan was an able, young warrior. Israel had many fighting men in its army. And God was with Saul. But in spite of those great advantages, Saul ultimately disobeyed God's command and it proved costly to himself, his family, and his country. Disobedience of one man does affect others. We do not live in isolation, and personal holiness and obedience to God matter, especially when we consider that our actions can and do affect those around us.

How does a lack of obedience on the part of God's people hurt the witness of believers today?

How can disobedience on the part of believers cause others to discount the gospel or avoid conversations about Christ?

The formation of Israel's monarchy led to renewal of the nation's conflict with the Philistines. The Philistines continued to be militarily superior. Furthermore, their monopoly on iron also provided them with economic advantages. Israel was a predominately agricultural society, but its farmers were totally dependent on Philistine blacksmiths for making and repairing tools needed for farming.

Saul's victory over the Ammonites (1 Sam. 11:5-11) encouraged action against the Philistines. Saul had divided his army and placed his son Jonathan in command of one force. Jonathan, an aggressive commander, quickly attacked a nearby Philistine outpost. The Philistines assembled a massive military force to crush Israel once and for all. Panic seized the Israelite army. Many soldiers deserted. Goaded by this widespread alarm, Saul usurped the role of priest and offered a sacrifice that displeased the Lord immensely. The prophet Samuel soundly denounced the king's rash action. The Philistine invaders sent three companies to attack the Israelites.

Displaying poor judgment, King Saul issued a rash vow that almost cost the life of his son. Nevertheless, the Philistine invasion was repulsed. Immediately thereafter, God instructed Saul to completely destroy the Amalekites. However, Saul failed to obey God fully. In this moment we can see how the actions of one person affect many others. As a result of Saul's disobedience to God, Saul and Samuel separated and never saw each other again. Even more significantly, God rejected Saul as king (1 Sam. 15:22-23). Saul's disobedience proved costly for him, his family, and the nation of Israel.

In what ways have you seen one person's disobedience affect someone else?

Read 1 Samuel 18:1-9; 19:11-17.

The root of jealousy is a belief that we deserve something better than what we have. This attitude not only displays a lack of gratitude, but challenges the wisdom and provision of God. We see how jealousy can turn a person to extreme choices through the life of Saul in 1 Samuel 18 and 19.

In the beginning, David and Saul had a good working relationship. David was a skilled commander and fighter, as well as the best friend of Saul's son Jonathan. Saul was initially pleased with David; David was not only loyal but also successful for the sake of Saul's kingdom. But soon Saul's attitude toward David soured.

Upon returning home from battle, the women offered their customary songs praising the men for their battles. Saul was praised for killing his thousands, and David was praised for killing his tens of thousands. Saul was jealous of David's praise and popularity, and it drove him mad. Jealousy caused Saul to ignore the blessing that David was to his kingdom. Saul intently focused on his own diminished level of popularity with the people. David's popularity and success in battle was evil in Saul's eyes. Saul connected the mention of David with Samuel's prophecy of a previously anonymous neighbor of Saul to whom the Lord had given the kingdom of Israel (see 1 Samuel 15:28). As a result, Saul watched David with jealousy.

Everyone experiences jealousy. As you think back through times when you have been jealous, are there any common threads or categories?

What are some of the more helpful things you have told yourself to overcome the temptations associated with jealousy?

Saul's jealousy impacted many more people than himself. What is the effect on a community of Christians when jealousy is present?

Saul's jealousy drove him mad, and he attempted to kill David on many occasions. Saul sent men to kill David when he left his house the next morning (1 Sam. 19:11). But Michal, David's wife, was aware of her father's plan and, like her brother, warned David of the danger and urged him to flee before morning (1 Sam. 19:2). She facilitated David's escape by letting him down through an unguarded window.

When his attempts to kill David failed, Saul had David followed and tried to use his daughter as a trap to keep David close. Saul's jealousy bubbled to the surface and eventually affected his kingdom and his family. Saul's family relationships and ability to govern came unraveled, all because he wanted what David had.

Was the issue of jealousy the whole problem? When we are jealous of another, what does that jealousy reveal about what we believe about God? About ourselves?

Our bigger problem is not with jealousy—it is with God, the One who decides who gets what. When we are jealous of another, we implicitly challenge the wisdom and generosity of God. Though we might try not to be jealous of what someone else has or does, we most need to be reminded of the goodness of God. As we are, our entitled heart will be transformed into a heart of gratitude, humility, and generosity. Instead of desiring what God has given to another, we will be able to truly celebrate His goodness all around us.

Read 1 Samuel 31.

The final chapter of 1 Samuel resumes the account of the Philistine war (1 Sam. 28–29). The Israelites were defeated and many were killed on Mount Gilboa. Saul, wounded severely by archers in the battle, tried to convince his terrified armor-bearer to run him through with a sword so that he could avoid torture by the Philistines, but the armor-bearer could not do it. Saul felt he had no choice other than to end his own life, and he fell on his own sword. His corpse was publicly abused by the Philistines. Three of Saul's sons were also killed in battle, which prepared the way for David to be king.

Saul's pride cultivated indifference to the will of God and jealousy of others, and eventually led to his shameful death. Yet despite the fact that Saul's legacy ended so poorly, the people of Jabesh-gilead remembered how Saul had delivered them from the Ammonites (11:1-11). They journeyed all night to Beth-shan, where Saul's body and those of his sons had been impaled. At great risk to themselves, they stole the bodies away and honorably buried them at Jabesh, where they mourned his death. Saul had not honored the people or the Lord well, but the people honored him as best they were able.

Have you ever attended the funeral of someone who, at the time of their death, was not living in obedience to the Lord? What are some of the things that you can think about and talk about with others in that situation?

How can you show honor to people who, in the times leading up to their death, were not showing honor to others? Why is it important to do this?

From the narrative, it appears that Saul died after three of his sons and may have even witnessed their deaths. You can only imagine the horror of Saul witnessing the brutal deaths of his children in large part due to his own hubris. All too frequently in his life,

Saul lived as if his preferences and choices had no negative consequences for anyone around him. Even with a prophet speaking directly to him as the voice of the Lord, Saul still believed he had at least some degree of sovereignty or control over his life's circumstances and could manipulate things in his favor.

How can you balance being responsible for your choices in life with the reality that you are not sovereign over your life?

When the people saw that Saul and his sons had been killed in battle, a mass desertion took place. This desertion speaks not of the soldiers, but of the citizens. When they saw the battle go against Israel, they fled their homes and cities and went across the Jordan to escape death. Many soldiers were doubtless in the crowd that fled the scene of battle, but the emphasis here is upon the citizens of the land. These people had earlier deserted the Lord to make Saul king, and then they deserted the land as consequences of Saul being king.

Overall, what lessons can be learned from this final chapter of King Saul's life?

DAVID

Israel's Humble King

INTRODUCTION

First impressions are easy to gain and difficult to lose. First impressions almost prevented David from becoming king of Israel.

God ordered the prophet Samuel to go to David's hometown of Bethlehem, approach the home of Jesse, and anoint the new king of Israel from among Jesse's many sons. How would the prophet recognize the new king? God would show him the man He had chosen. But it would not keep Samuel from trying to guess which one of Jesse's sons was going to be king. Samuel probably guessed based on the same factors we would use today—the person's height, strength, and beauty—in essence, his outward appearance. But Samuel was wrong, and he was pleasantly surprised at God's choice for the new king.

David was called because of God's sovereign choice. The new king was chosen from a working-class family in a small town called Bethlehem. The new king was just a young man, a shepherd, and not someone who had worked his way up to the position. He was simply chosen by God. David had no clue that his life was about to change so dramatically. He was simply carrying out his responsibilities, faithfully serving his family.

David's kingship was unparalleled. Some have called him the greatest leader the world has ever known. While by no means perfect, by and large David's life can be summarized in one word: humility. For this reason and others, David is considered one of the great leaders and servants of Scripture.

How does pride lead to ruin? How does humility lead to honor?

Watch the video teaching for Session 2 to discover "The World of King David," then continue the group discussion.

GROUP DISCUSSION

Focus Attention

List some qualities people look for in a person who is going to lead a nation. What is the most important quality in your mind?

Explore The Text

As a group, read 1 Samuel 16:1-10.

God led the prophet Samuel to anoint Saul as Israel's first king (see 1 Sam. 8–9). However, in 1 Samuel 15, Samuel told Saul that because of his disobedience, the kingdom would be taken from him and given to someone else. The new person God picked to be anointed as king was chosen based upon an entirely different criteria than we might expect.

Is God impressed by the same qualities that impress us? Why or why not?

Why did Samuel initially think Eliab was the Lord's choice? What's the irony here (see 1 Sam. 10:23-24)?

What does verse 7 suggest about the qualities God counts as most important for His servants?

Eliab evidently had the physical features of a star actor or athlete, looking every bit the part of a potential king. As Jesse's oldest son stood before him, Samuel must have compared him with the tall and impressive Saul (1 Sam. 10:23-24). Our culture also evaluates people by their appearance, social status, and other superficial traits. Nevertheless, people do not see what God sees. Outward appearances often deceive people, but they never deceive God.

As a group, read 1 Samuel 16:11-13.

What characteristic would seem to hinder David from being anointed as king (v. 11)?

What did David's faithfulness in watching the sheep say about his character? How did this prepare him for the future (see 1 Sam. 17:34-37; Ps. 23)?

David's faithful work as a shepherd reminds us of two important truths. First, it doesn't matter what we do, but how we do it. No matter what tasks we are given, we are to do them in a way that brings glory to God. Second, we learn that God is working behind the scenes in David's life in order to prepare him for his future role as king. Tending sheep helped prepare David to rule Israel. "Shepherd" would become a symbolic job description for king. God intended for the king to care for people with the same compassion that a shepherd gives to the flock. Also, David's encounters with predators developed skills that later became useful in combat.

Reflecting on this passage as a whole, what qualified David to be king? Why did God choose David?

APPLY THE TEXT

Throughout the Bible, God chose unlikely people to join Him in His plans to redeem humanity from sin. You may not think of yourself as a likely candidate to lead anything of a spiritual nature. Perhaps you've even said no to opportunities to provide needed leadership at your church. But the Bible is full of people with less than perfect backgrounds. It seems that these are the kinds of people God chooses—broken, imperfect, yet full of promise when they seek forgiveness, strive to do God's will, repent of past mistakes, and move on in the grace only God can provide.

Who do you identify with most in this story—Samuel, Jesse, Jesse's sons, or David? Why?

How might knowing that God has chosen you to serve Him change the way that you view your occupation or role in life?

Close your group time in prayer, reflecting on what you have discussed.

DAVID

KEY VERSES

The Spirit of the LORD spoke through me, his word was on my tongue. The God of Israel spoke; the Rock of Israel said to me, "The one who rules the people with justice, who rules in the fear of God, is like the morning light when the sun rises on a cloudless morning, the glisten of rain on sprouting grass."

— 2 Samuel 23:2-4

BASIC FACTS

1. Youngest son of Jesse of Bethlehem, who became Israel's second king and the most revered Israelite ruler in history.

2. Name *David* means "beloved."

3. Anointed at a young age by the prophet Samuel to become king in place of Saul; became king at age thirty.

4. Ruled as king forty years; seven years over Judah, thirty-three years in Jerusalem over all Israel.

5. Married eight wives with whom he had eleven children (ten sons, one daughter); had nine other sons by concubines.

6. Died at age seventy and buried in Jerusalem.

TIMELINE

1100–1050 BC

- Samuel 1105–1025
- Saul 1080–1010
- Death of Eli, priest at Shiloh 1070
- Twenty-first Dynasty in Egypt 1069–945
- Samson defeats enemies in death at Gaza 1060

1050–1000 BC

- Saul chosen as first king of Israel 1050
- David 1040–970
- David becomes king of Judah 1010
- David becomes king of all Israel 1003

KNOWN FOR

1. Young and armed with only a sling and stones, David challenged and killed Goliath, a giant Philistine warrior, by trusting in the Lord to give him the victory (1 Sam. 17).

2. David had to spend years as a bandit leader in hiding from King Saul, who was determined to kill David (1 Sam. 20-27).

3. After David became king of all Israel, he moved the ark of God to Jerusalem and made plans to build a temple to house it. God stopped David's plans, but made a covenant with the king to establish David's kingdom forever (2 Sam. 6-7).

4. David committed adultery with Bathsheba, the wife of one of his loyal soldiers; then he tried to cover up his sin by ensuring that the husband and soldier (Uriah) was killed in battle (2 Sam. 11).

5. He married Bathsheba and the couple had a son, Solomon, who later succeeded David as king (2 Sam. 12:24; 1 Kings 1:32-35).

6. David wrote and collected many psalms; known as the "sweet psalmist of Israel" (2 Sam. 23:1; KJV).

7. He is remembered as the ideal king and forerunner of the Messiah (Isa. 9:6-7; Luke 1:30-33).

1000–950 BC

- Chinese store ice for refrigeration 1000
- David conquers Jerusalem; moves ark 1000
- Absalom revolts against David 975
- Solomon 990–931
- David dies; Solomon anointed king 970
- Temple of Solomon completed 959

950–900 BC

- Hezion (Rezon) rules in Syria 940–915
- Solomon dies; Rehoboam becomes king 931
- Israel splits into two kingdoms 931
- Rehoboam rules Southern Kingdom 931–913
- Shishak (Egypt) invades Jerusalem 926–917
- Jeroboam I rules Northern Kingdom 931–909
- Jeroboam I erects golden calf idols 925

David's Desire: A Clean Heart

By Bryan E. Beyer

In Psalm 51:10, King David pleaded with God to give him a "clean heart." The psalm's heading refers to David's adultery with Bathsheba. When Bathsheba became pregnant, David arranged for her husband Uriah's death to cover his own sin.

God's prophet Nathan confronted David. God had blessed David incredibly, but David had violated God's law. Israel's king at last came to repentance and experienced God's forgiveness, but sin's consequences haunted him the rest of his life.

Writing Psalm 51, David poured out his heart to God. He prayed for restoration and confessed his transgressions. Finally, David offered thanksgiving to God as he looked to a day when restoration would come to David and to Jerusalem (see vv. 13-19).

Psalm 51:10 contains rich theological words that reflect the depth of David's plea. The Hebrew word *bara* ("create") describes God's creative power in making the heavens and earth (see Gen. 1:1,21,27; 2:3). David needed God to re-order his life after he strayed so far from Him.

The word *tahor* ("clean") denotes a moral cleanliness. Under the Law of Moses, people often brought sacrifices or offerings to the Lord as a demonstration of their desire for purity, but the offering itself did not purify the worshiper. God ultimately desired inner purity and cleanliness over an external sacrifice.

The word *leb* ("heart") represented the seat of one's intellect, emotion, and will. The heart guided people to make the right decisions, but David's heart had become spiritually hardened. He had to humble himself to experience God's mercy and grace.

The word *chadash* ("renew") means to refresh or restore something that already exists. David wanted God's help to start over with a renewed heart and spirit.

The word *nakhon* ("steadfast") was often used in a spiritual or moral sense to denote firmness of belief, conviction, or attitude. David used it to describe his own heart that was confidently established in the Lord when David was hiding from King Saul (Ps. 57:7, "confident"). How he had strayed from that attitude!

Bryan E. Beyer, "David's Desire: A Clean Heart," *Biblical Illustrator*, Summer 2017.

The word *ruach* ("spirit") denoted David's moral character. He also used this word to describe the "broken spirit" God desired (v. 17). David's brokenness would please God more than any sacrifice he could bring.

The ancient Hebrews naturally would have interpreted David's plea through what they knew of the Law of Moses. Sinners normally brought sacrifices as expressions of their sorrow and repentance. At the same time, David's cry for an internal change of heart and mind would have provided a powerful example of the life God truly wanted. Later prophets, such as Isaiah and Micah, echoed this theme: God had much more delight in faithful obedience and humble brokenness than in offerings that did not express a contrite heart (see Isa. 1:11-15; Mic. 6:6-8).

In Amman, Jordan, visitors approach the ruins of a Byzantine church, which was constructed inside what had been the citadel at ancient Ammon. Uriah the Hittite was killed while storming the citadel at Ammon.

Illustrator Photo/ Bob Schatz (8/4/9)

Read 1 Samuel 16:1-13.

God is sovereign, which means that He is the absolute authority in life—He has the right to make any decision that is consistent with His perfect character. God's choice of a new leader for Israel was David, which made David God's sovereign choice. As we will discover later, David would grow up, mature, and become a great king and leader. He would not be a perfect king and leader. Far from it. But he was still God's choice to lead.

Who is one of the greatest leaders you've known or known about? Why is that person your choice?

David's arrival at his father's house was accompanied by the only physical description that is given of him. In one translation of Scripture, David is described as being "ruddy." From the Hebrew, that means "dark, reddened complexion." Some commentaries say that David had red hair. However, the description isn't that he had red hair, but that he was of reddened complexion.

The description also indicates he had good countenance. That is an internal description. Countenance emanates from the inside and is reflected on the outside. There are a lot of good-looking people who do not have good countenance.

Scripture also indicates he was handsome. Nevertheless, David was not God's choice because of his looks, but because of his love—not because he was handsome, but because of his heart. However, we shouldn't miss the fact that all of Jesse's sons were good-looking men. The hint of the narrative is that Samuel was impressed with all of them, and would have been delighted to pour the oil out on any of them.

God's choice of David was based on his inner qualities, not his outer qualities. With the confirming words of God, "Anoint him, for he is the one" (v. 12), Samuel again uncorked the horn and poured the oil on David's head, signifying that he was God's choice to be leader and king.

What emotions or thoughts do you have knowing that God looks past our outward appearance and instead evaluates us based on our heart and character?

Who in your life saw inner potential in you and was a source of encouragement?

This must have been the occasion David reflected on to write Psalm 23:5, "You anoint my head with oil; my cup overflows." In the same space that describes the anointing in 1 Samuel, it says, "The Spirit of the LORD came powerfully on David from that day forward" (16:13).

This was mentioned because the position of king over Israel was, first and foremost, a spiritual position, which was not the case with the other neighboring kings. David needed spiritual resources to be king over God's people.

David's appointment wasn't instant. Many years passed between the time of David's anointing and the day he would officially become king. Instead, his anointing was a promise from God that one day David would lead Israel and be its king. David was God's choice.

Could God choose you to be a leader? Has he already done so and you're resisting because you don't feel worthy? Remember that God looks past who the world sees, and He sees the person we can become in relationship with Him. He knows our potential to be used by Him to do great things. God chose David. He may be choosing you too.

Read 1 Samuel 18:1-4; 19:4-7; 20:8,12-13.

If you created a list of your five closest friends, who would be on that list? If you could add ten more names of acquaintances, who would you include? Many adults have a handful of very close friends, but many more acquaintances. To make such a list of close friends might include immediate family and coworkers. However, a list of acquaintances is much longer.

Is the act of forming deep friendships today easier or more difficult than twenty years ago? Why do you believe this to be so?

How do you find that "best friend" we all need? How do you become a best friend to someone else?

The Bible teaches us the importance of having friends (see Prov. 17:17; 18:24; 27:9). Unfortunately, we live in a society where many adults like the support they receive from friends, but they do little to provide the benefits of friendship for others. Godly friendships involve mutual support and benefits based on a common allegiance to God.

A relationship of mutual support describes the friendship between David and Saul's son, Jonathan. Their story affirms the value of having godly friends. It is important to discover ways we can cultivate godly friendships.

How have you been a friend to someone recently? What benefit did you receive by being a friend?

The web of relationships formed around Saul and David was remarkably complex. Saul's insecurities led Saul to sometimes "need" David, yet other times despise and envy him. At one point, Saul offered his daughter Merab to David as his wife if David would continue to fight Saul's enemies. Saul hoped David would be killed in battle. David insisted he did not deserve the king's daughter, but another of Saul's daughters named Michal fell in love with David, so Saul offered her hand in marriage in exchange for the deaths of one hundred Philistines. David killed two hundred of the enemy and married Michal, a move that only further incensed Saul.

To complicate matters further, David's best friend was Saul's son, Jonathan. Jonathan knew that Saul intended to kill David, so he spoke up in David's defense and intervened to protect David from Saul. In all of this, David was challenged to respect the authority and office of the kingship, maintain loyalty to a dear friend, and love his wife. No small feat!

Have you ever found yourself in a similarly complicated web of relationships? What challenges are associated with balancing them?

Practically speaking, what is the difference between honoring other people and pleasing other people? Which did David do, and why?

Read 1 Samuel 24:1-7a,11-12,16-22.

Christians often sense a conflict between their values and those promoted in some segments of contemporary culture. For example, retaliation seems to be a widely accepted practice when we feel like justice can't be served any other way, but Christians are committed to letting the Lord mete out justice. In this story, David had an opportunity to exact revenge against Saul for attempting to kill him, but David chose to abide by the Lord's commands.

What is the hardest part about not taking action against someone who has harmed you?

Instead of killing Saul when he was defenseless, David cut off a piece of Saul's robe. David's men saw Saul's arrival in the cave as the fulfillment of some sort of prophecy. David, they thought, should take advantage of this opportunity to kill Saul.

When have you been tempted to take action against someone, only to relent and show that person mercy? What feelings did you have after you made that decision?

Although David acted with mercy toward Saul, he soon regretted even cutting his robe and told his followers he would never hurt God's anointed king. When David announced to Saul that he had spared his life, Saul declared David more righteous than himself. David took an oath not to attack Saul's family. David's speech persuaded his men, and none of them tried to kill Saul either.

David's decision is puzzling for many. We live in a world in which revenge and retaliation are not only exercised but expected. Clearly David's decision was motivated by something higher than the morals of the day. It can only be explained by faith that God had put Saul in his position and, therefore, should be respected.

How do we show respect to people we disagree with yet who hold leadership roles in our workplace, church, or country?

David knew that vengeance was the Lord's. He did not need to take the situation into his own hands. He trusted that God's justice would remedy the alienation between the present king and the future king.

Likewise, we can trust that God will right every wrong done to us. As Christians, we must forgive our enemies and pray for them. By trying to exact revenge, we really declare that we do not trust in a sovereign, all-powerful God to judge and punish wrongdoers. We have no need to take action against those who persecute us; instead, we can leave that in God's hands, trusting that He is a righteous judge who knows our hearts, sees our actions, and brings wrongdoers to justice. David knew this well and lived by his belief in a God who makes all things right. We can do the same.

To whom could you show mercy, even though this person may be wrong in his or her actions or words toward you?

SOLOMON

Israel's Wise King

INTRODUCTION

Life is filled with incredibly difficult choices, and from a variety of fields. While we might feel capable of making some of these choices, others expose the fact that we simply cannot know everything we need to know in order to choose rightly. That is, we lack wisdom. Thankfully, God delights in giving us wisdom to live rightly and help others in every area of our lives.

In his dying instructions to his son Solomon, King David charged the new king to obey God's law and to punish David's enemies. When God asked Solomon what gift he would like, Solomon responded with a request for great wisdom to lead God's people. God granted the request. And more.

Solomon showed himself to be an unusually wise king who, for much of his reign, was concerned with staying humble, ruling his people according to God's ways, and maintaining a strong personal relationship with God. When we sincerely ask God to direct our lives as Solomon did, we often must re-prioritize our lives and make many choices, some difficult.

Who is the wisest person you know?

To whom do you turn when you need someone to help you make an important decision?

Watch the video teaching for Session 3 to discover "The World of King Solomon," then continue the group discussion.

FOCUS ATTENTION

Where do people turn to get wisdom today? Why might these sources of human wisdom fall short and disappoint the person asking for help?

EXPLORE THE TEXT

As a group, read 1 Kings 3:1-9.

How do you suppose you would respond to God if He said to you, "Ask. What should I give you?" Explain.

Why did Solomon desire wisdom above anything else? What does this reveal about him and his relationship with God?

What situation in your life right now makes you feel inadequate? What difference has God's wisdom made in how you have (or have not) dealt with that situation?

As a group, read 1 Kings 3:10-15.

Why did Solomon's request please God? Can you think of another request that would have pleased God more than the desire for wisdom?

What does God's willingness to give Solomon more than he asked for reveal about His nature? How have you witnessed God's generosity in your own life?

God was pleased that Solomon's request centered on the successful accomplishment of God's calling and not on worldly or self-centered desires. God listed three requests a self-focused king might have made in Solomon's situation: long life, riches, or the death of enemies. God promised to give Solomon a wise and understanding heart. He granted Solomon's request above and beyond what was asked, beginning with the kind of "heart" that would equip Solomon to rule effectively and justly over God's people.

Because Solomon asked for things on behalf of God's people (see 3:9), God gave the honor and prestige of a worthy monarch.

APPLY THE TEXT

Even though Solomon did not ask for riches, God gave him riches along with the requested wisdom. God does not promise to give you wealth, but He does promise to meet all your needs. God wants you to put Him first in your life, to fill your mind with His desires, to imitate Him, and to serve and obey Him in everything. Then He will give you what you need from day to day.

Evaluate your priorities in light of Solomon's. In what ways do you value living with godly wisdom more than pursuing personal wealth or achievements?

What are some blessings that might accompany God-given wisdom, and how might you use such blessings in God's service?

Close your group time in prayer, reflecting on what you have discussed.

SOLOMON

KEY VERSES

LORD my God, you have now made your servant king in my father David's place. Yet I am just a youth with no experience in leadership. . . . So give your servant a receptive heart to judge your people and to discern between good and evil. For who is able to judge this great people of yours?

— 1 Kings 3:7,9

BASIC FACTS

1. Son of David and Bathsheba who succeeded his father as king of Israel and greatly extended Israel's influence in the ancient world.

2. Name *Solomon* relates to the Hebrew word for "peace" (shalom).

3. Also known as *Jedidiah*, meaning "beloved of Yahweh," a name given him at birth by Nathan the prophet.

4. Reigned as king of Israel for forty years.

5. His age at death not indicated in Scripture but estimated to be around age sixty.

TIMELINE

1050–1000 BC
Saul chosen as first king of Israel 1050
David 1040–970
David becomes king of Judah 1010
David becomes king of all Israel 1003

1000–950 BC
Chinese store ice for refrigeration 1000
David conquers Jerusalem; moves ark 1000
Absalom revolts against David 975
Solomon 990–931
David dies; Solomon anointed king 970
Temple of Solomon completed 959

KNOWN FOR

----

1. Early in his reign, Solomon prayed for God to give him wisdom to rule, a request God granted along with great wealth and world influence (1 Kings 3:10-14).

2. His renown for wisdom included difficult judicial decisions (1 Kings 3:16-28), literary works (three thousand proverbs and over one thousand songs/psalms; 1 Kings 4:32), and administrative skills (1 Kings 4:1-28).

3. Solomon engaged in great building projects, including a palace complex and, more significantly, the temple of the Lord (1 Kings 5–7). To complete these projects, he expanded the use of slave labor (1 Kings 9:15-23).

4. Solomon famously "wowed" the queen of Sheba with his wisdom and wealth to the extent that she gave him unmatched gifts of gold and spices, and he gave the queen "her every desire—whatever she asked" (1 Kings 10:1-13).

5. He extended Israel's dominance over surrounding kingdoms further than any Israelite ruler before or after him (1 Kings 4:20-21).

6. Solomon had a harem of seven hundred wives and three hundred concubines, which included an Egyptian Pharaoh's daughter (1 Kings 7:8). Solomon's foreign wives persuaded him to establish idol worship in Israel, angering God (1 Kings 11:1-10).

7. In his later years, Solomon developed serious questions about life's ultimate meaning. He recorded his struggles regarding the seeming futility of life in the Book of Ecclesiastes.

950-900 BC

- Solomon dies; Rehoboam becomes king 931
- Israel splits into two kingdoms 931
- Rehoboam rules Southern Kingdom 931–913
- Shishak (Egypt) invades Jerusalem 926–917
- Jeroboam I rules Northern Kingdom 931–910
- Jeroboam I erects golden calf idols 925
- Asa reigns in Judah 911–870

900-850 BC

- First temple reform under Asa 897
- Omri (Israel) makes Samaria his capital 880
- Ahab reigns in Northern Kingdom 874–853
- Elijah's prophetic ministry 862–852
- Shalmaneser III becomes king in Assyria 859
- Ben-hadad (Syria) attacks Samaria 857

Solomon: All We Know

By Duane A. Garrett

Solomon ruled Israel approximately 970-931 BC. He was the second son of David and Bathsheba. Their first son died as punishment for David's sin (see 2 Sam. 12:14-24). David's fourth son was Adonijah (see 3:4); he considered himself the legitimate heir to the throne. As David was dying, Adonijah attempted to seize power preemptively and thus block any rival claims. But Nathan the prophet, Zadok the priest, and Bathsheba persuaded David to proclaim that his heir and co-ruler was Solomon (see 1 Kings 1). After David's death, Solomon showed himself ferociously decisive in dealing with opposition.

The Bible reports little concerning geopolitical events from Solomon's reign; but it does speak of his domestic, cultural, diplomatic, and commercial achievements. Solomon reorganized the state (see 4:1-19); developed a large, modern military (see 4:26-28); and engaged in a massive building program. The centerpiece project of his administration was the construction of the temple (see chs. 5–7). Solomon promoted an intellectual renaissance. He composed proverbs and songs, and he had a keen interest in natural history (see 4:29-34). Solomon enjoyed good relations with the outer world—including Egypt, the Arabian kingdom of Sheba (see 10:1-10), and the mercantile Phoenician city of Tyre (see 5:1). He engaged in extensive trading ventures (see 9:26-28; 10:11,23-29). Solomon's kingdom was wealthy, extensive, and secure. The people enjoyed a level of prosperity they had never experienced before and would never know again (see 4:25).

Solomon loved Yahweh, but he also sacrificed at the high places (see 3:3). Solomon's piety is most evident in his request for wisdom from God (see 3:4-15), and in his dedicatory prayer at the Temple's inaugural ceremony (see 8:14-61). His wisdom and discernment, as illustrated in biblical anecdotes (see 3:16-28; 10:1-10), indicate he had a strong moral center. For all that, however, Solomon was in many respects a moral and spiritual failure. Deuteronomy 17:16-17 forbids the Israelite king from engaging in certain activities. These prohibitions, though, make for a virtual biography of Solomon.

Duane A. Garrett, "Solomon: All We Know," *Biblical Illustrator*, Spring 2014.

From the standpoint of the narrator of 1 Kings, Solomon's greatest moral failure was building pagan sanctuaries. The text attributes this sin to Solomon's foreign wives' influence and implies that as Solomon got older, he became increasingly apostate (see 11:1-8). As far as we can tell, Solomon never attempted to undo the damage done by these shrines to foreign gods and by the burdens he placed on the people.

Christians struggle to reconcile this with the notion that Solomon wrote several biblical books, particularly Proverbs. One solution is that he wrote the canonical books while he was more orthodox, and there is no doubt truth in this. Almost certainly, though, he was never entirely free of pagan thinking. Solomon was never averse to dealing with pagans, even to the point of contracting out the building of the temple to a pagan king. The best analysis may be that he was indeed wise and devout but had some enormous blind spots, and that God used him in spite of his failings.

Solomonic gate and casemate walls at Hazor in northern Israel. First Kings 9:15 refers to the "forced labor that King Solomon had imposed to build the LORD's temple, his own palace, the supporting terraces, the wall of Jerusalem, and Hazor, Megiddo, and Gezer" (CSB).

Illustrator Photo/ Bob Schatz (19-7-19)

Read 1 Kings 3:16-28.

Solomon's new-found wisdom would soon be tested by two prostitutes. This story is one of the best known in the whole Bible. Israel's kings were sometimes called upon to settle particularly hard cases (see 2 Sam 12:1-6; 14:1-11), and this situation is quite perplexing.

Two prostitutes had given birth to babies. One woman smothered her child in the night, then switched babies while the other woman slept. Now both women claimed the living child as their own. Without other witnesses or evidence, Solomon had to devise some way to solve the case, exercise wisdom, and provide justice.

When have you been called on to make a difficult decision? How did you decide on a course of action?

Kings were the highest recourse for justice, expected to be in a place of public access to take up the case of the widow, the orphan, and the oppressed. Solomon quickly produced his own evidence. He decided to try the case based on the women's maternal instincts and human compassion. Calling for a sword, he ordered the child cut in two, with each woman getting an equal share. The real mother, who already cared enough for her child to plead her case before the king, acted out of "compassion for her son." She begged Solomon to give the baby to the other woman so that the child could live. In startling contrast, the dishonest woman was willing to take her "half." Her cruelty was revealed, just as the other mother's kindness emerged.

What are the most common sources of wisdom you turn to when you face difficult decisions or judgment calls? Would those sources have helped you in this scenario? Why or why not?

There was obviously a lot of animosity between the two women, not surprising in the circumstances in which they lived. Solomon's judgment did not deal with the circumstances of the death of the child or with the various accusations being made. His concern was with the bonding relationship of a mother and her child, which he presumed to be present by virtue of the fact that the case had come before him. The living child had no father, but the true mother was determined to care for her child and to give it hope in this world.

Faced with the horror of watching her child die, the emotions of the true mother compelled her to acquiesce to the demands of her wicked associate (see v. 26). Once Solomon knew the identity of the true mother, he did not engage in further punishments, either to deal with the cause of the first death or the subsequent criminal actions in switching the children. Solomon was then able to deliver a just verdict. The compassionate woman was given the child. He had the insight to see the difference between just and unjust persons even when he had no corroborating evidence.

When this verdict became public knowledge, the nation revered their king (v. 28). This respect stemmed from the knowledge that wisdom like Solomon's could come only from God. Israel now understood that "God's wisdom was in him to carry out justice." If so, the nation would flourish under his leadership.

What decision or situation are you facing in which you could use the kind of wisdom Solomon demonstrated?

Read 1 Kings 8:22-43.

Solomon started the foundation of the temple in Jerusalem during the fourth year of his reign. The structure required seven years, intense manpower, and much money to finish.

Eleven months after its completion, during the symbolic Festival of Booths, Solomon assembled Israel's leadership in Jerusalem where he held a national ceremony to dedicate the temple and rededicate the nation to God. He had the ark of the Lord's covenant brought into the temple. The priests placed the ark in the inner sanctuary, the most holy place. God's glory filled the building in the form of a cloud, giving the people a visible manifestation of His presence and showing His approval of the temple.

Having encouraged the people by stressing God's past saving acts (vv. 12-21), Solomon next began the process of asking the Lord in prayer to save Israel in the future (vv. 22-43).

According to 1 Kings 8:23, what is it about God that motivates Him to love and keep a people for Himself?

How does the character of God determine the nature and content of our prayers?

One might conclude that a god worthy of such a temple operated out of obligation or guilt. Solomon's prayer reveals that the one true God relates to His people in an entirely different kind of way. Not obligation, not legalism, nor a desire to control others for personal gain motivates God. Every miracle, saving act, or law flows from divine mercy and grace. It's for this reason that Solomon understood God stands ready to hear people's prayers, to forgive their sins, and to initiate or restore their relationship with Him. He hears those who pour out their needs and problems to Him.

In your current walk with the Lord, are you motivated to pray? Why or why not? What characteristics of God highlighted in Solomon's prayer stand out to you in this moment?

What keeps you from the discipline of prayer? What can you do about distractions and interruptions?

Solomon's prayer reveals a few things about God that motivate us to pray and inform the nature and content of our prayers.

- God is faithful to keep His promises.
- God listens to our prayers.
- God responds to our prayers by forgiving us and acting to help us.

How different prayer would be if God were not faithful, a good listener, responsive, or forgiving! May these attributes of God inspire and motivate us to pray to a loving and faithful God who longs for a relationship with His people!

Read 1 Kings 11:1-13.

When it comes to resolving conflict, compromise by all parties is often required. Finding common ground heals broken relationships. It can restore diplomatic relations between feuding nations. It can reduce disagreements between husbands and wives. Reaching a win-win solution can make friendships stronger. Spiritual compromise, however, is always wrong. When we ignore God's clear statements of right and wrong, we sin. God holds Christians accountable for their sins regardless of position, age, or previous faithfulness.

Based on external appearances, King Solomon achieved great success as a ruler. People recognized him as a man of great wisdom. The king completed extensive building projects and accumulated great wealth. He expanded David's kingdom and established peaceful relations with the surrounding nations.

Despite his outward achievements, however, Solomon failed in his personal life. Moral and spiritual weaknesses increasingly characterized the end of his life and rule. He failed to honor God and keep love for Him above his own desires. Solomon's mistakes had disastrous results for his family and the nation. God held Solomon accountable for his sins and judged him for his disobedience. His negative example encourages us to guard against any spiritual compromise.

Compare Solomon's actions with Deuteronomy 7:1-4; 17:17. What specific commands did Solomon disobey?

Solomon's spiritual downfall started with a departure from God's laws. He forfeited wholehearted love for God and obedience to Him. One compromise led to another.

What role did Solomon's wives play in his idolatry? What can you learn from Solomon's example about the influence of others on your spiritual life?

Tolerating idolatry within his own household eventually led to Solomon's own participation in idolatry. What does this teach us about sin?

Solomon's tragic end is puzzling. This king had much going for him, but he seemed to waste it by giving in to his own desires. The Lord blessed him with more than he asked. He had a glorious kingdom, riches, wisdom, and fame. Yet Solomon allowed sin to remain all around him, and it eventually corrupted him. He started with a good foundation, but he did not remain faithful to God. His small compromises led to great sins. His impressive accomplishments were overshadowed by his unimpressive character.

In what detail of your life do you know you are consciously and willfully disobeying a direct command from God?

What steps do you need to take to remain faithful to God and avoid spiritual compromise?

ASA
Israel's Idol-Destroying King

INTRODUCTION

Does your family determine your destiny?

Thankfully, the answer to that question is "No."

Asa's father, Abijah, and his grandfather, Rehoboam, were sinful men who led Judah away from the Lord. The queen mother (it is uncertain, but apparently she was his grandmother) was a shame to him and the nation, setting up a horrid image of Asherah, a Canaanite goddess.

From this lineage, you might expect King Asa to be a horrible person. Yet we are told in 2 Chronicles 14:2, "Asa did good and right in the sight of the LORD his God."

Asa reigned for forty-one years as one of Judah's most godly kings. He was a reformer, leading the Southern Kingdom back to the worship of the one true God. So effective were his reforms that many from Israel (the northern ten tribes) defected to his kingdom and joined in the revival of his days. At the end, however, Asa stumbled, and the last five years of his reign were out of step with the godliness that had characterized it up to that point. The civil war with Israel resurfaced, and instead of trusting God, Asa trusted in an alliance with the pagan king of Aram.

What are some qualities or habits you have inherited from your parents or grandparents?

How is your life similar to, or different from, the lives lived by your parents and grandparents?

Watch the video teaching for Session 4 to discover "The World of King Asa," then continue the group discussion.

FOCUS ATTENTION

Have you ever felt the need to make a clean break with your past? Explain.

EXPLORE THE TEXT

As a group, read 2 Chronicles 14:1-5.

What is the author's theological assessment of Asa's reign overall? How did Asa's faithfulness impact the everyday lives of the people?

Note the phrase "seek the Lord" in verse 4. What does it look like at a very practical level for people, both individually and corporately, to seek the Lord? What is the effect on both?

For those in Asa's day, the phrase "seek the Lord" described how one was to respond to God, and thus defined one who was a member of the believing community. It involved more than a specific act of seeking God's help and guidance but stood for one's whole duty toward God. In other words, it is knowing God and being wholeheartedly devoted to Him. In Asa's time, this meant in part repentance from idol worship and the destruction of all that might have been a representation of that worship.

What forms of idol worship are prevalent in our culture today? What is appealing about them? What specific dangers to they pose to Christians?

Why do you think we so easily fall into the trap of giving our hearts to idols? What are some of the excuses we use when rationalizing our emotional connection to idols?

Asa was said to have removed the high places from all the cities of Judah. Why is it important to be thorough when we begin to remove things that distract us from worshiping the true and living God?

APPLY THE TEXT

The "good and right" that Asa did was to remove the foreign (Canaanite) altars, high places, sacred pillars, and the Asherim. Not only did he remove the negative influences of Baal worship, but Asa also commanded Judah to seek the Lord and study His Word (the Law). As a result of Asa's "clean-up" campaign, the land was undisturbed for ten years, and, instead of putting their energies into war, they were able to build the nation's infrastructure. Out of such a family one would hardly expect an Asa. Yet God in His faithfulness raised up a man with a heart for Him.

In what ways have you allowed your family background to keep you from serving the Lord? Based on Asa's example, is there any reason you could not make a break with the past and choose to begin serving the Lord today? Explain.

At its root meaning, idolatry is the worship of created things in place of the worship of Creator God. What created things are most tempting for you to worship or idolize: Money? Pleasure? Food? Toys? Work? Yourself? Why are you tempted by those things?

What does a life that truly has God in the primary place of worship look like? What are some of the key characteristics of this lifestyle?

Close your group time in prayer, reflecting on what you have discussed.

ASA

KEY VERSE

Then Asa cried out to the LORD his God: "LORD, there is no one besides you to help the mighty and those without strength. Help us, LORD our God, for we depend on you, and in your name we have come against this large army. LORD, you are our God. Do not let a mere mortal hinder you."

— 2 Chronicles 14:11

BASIC FACTS

1. Great-grandson of Solomon, who succeeded his father Abijam (or Abijah) as ruler of the Southern Kingdom of Judah in 911 BC.

2. Name *Asa* means "physician" or "healing."

3. Reigned forty-one years as king.

4. Married to Azubah, who gave birth to Asa's son and successor, Jehoshaphat.

5. Developed severe foot disease two years before his death.

6. Buried in a tomb he made for himself in Jerusalem.

TIMELINE

1000–950 BC

- Chinese store ice for refrigeration 1000
- David conquers Jerusalem; moves ark 1000
- Absalom revolts against David 975
- Solomon 990–931
- David dies; Solomon anointed king 970
- Temple of Solomon completed 959

950–900 BC

- Solomon dies; Rehoboam becomes king 931
- Israel splits into two kingdoms 931
- Rehoboam rules Southern Kingdom 931–913
- Shishak (Egypt) invades Jerusalem 926–917
- Jeroboam I rules Northern Kingdom 931–910
- Jeroboam I erects golden calf idols 925
- Asa reigns in Judah 911–870

KNOWN FOR

1. Asa led Judah in a national movement of repentance and renewal. The movement included the removal of pagan altars, idols, and shrines, as well as the rebuilding of fortifications around key cities to protect against foreign invaders (2 Chron. 14:2-7; 15:1-19).

2. Asa deposed his grandmother, Maacah, from her royal position as the queen mother because she was an idol worshiper and had erected an obscene idol to the Canaanite goddess Asherah (1 Kings 15:13).

3. Threatened by an invasion from the south of a million-man army of Cushites, King Asa sought the Lord's help and repelled the invaders with his much smaller army of 300,000 warriors (2 Chron. 14:8-15).

4. In the thirty-sixth year of Asa's reign, the king of the Northern Kingdom declared war on Judah. Instead of seeking the Lord's help, Asa made an alliance with the king of Aram (Syria) to attack his rival from the north. While Asa succeeded in forcing the Northern Kingdom to withdraw, the king received a prophetic rebuke for not trusting in the Lord (2 Chron. 16:1-10).

5. Asa's lack of trust in the Lord continued when he developed a severe foot disease. Whether the disease cut short the king's life is unclear, but he sought help only from physicians and not from God (2 Chron. 16:12-13).

900-850 BC

- First temple reform under Asa 897
- Omri (Israel) makes Samaria his capital 880
- Ahab reigns in Northern Kingdom 874-853
- Jehoshaphat rules in Judah 872-848
- Elijah's prophetic ministry 862-852
- Shalmaneser III becomes king in Assyria 859
- Ben-hadad (Syria) attacks Samaria 857

850-800 BC

- Elisha's prophetic ministry 850-798
- Athaliah's reign of terror in Judah 841-835
- Jehu's reign in Northern Kingdom 841-814
- Joel's prophetic ministry (early date) 836-796
- Second temple reform under Joash 812

Asa: Success & Failure

By George H. Shaddix

Asa, the third king of Judah, reigned 910–869 BC, after the division of the kingdom of Israel into the kingdoms of Judah and Israel. Early in his reign, Asa expelled the male cultic prostitutes from the land. He removed the idols that his father had made and the high places and altars from every town in Judah. Additionally, Asa removed his grandmother Maacah as queen mother because of her idolatry.

Asa brought silver, gold, and other articles into the temple in Jerusalem. He also fortified the cities of Judah. These years were a time of prosperity.

The first military battle during Asa's reign occurred when Zerah the Cushite attacked Judah. With his army outnumbered, Asa prayed to the Lord for help. With God's help, Asa and the nation of Judah successfully defeated Zerah's forces (see 2 Chron. 14).

After the battle, a prophet named Azariah reminded Asa and all the people that as long as they followed the Lord, He would be with them. Asa was encouraged by the prophet's words and continued the reforms he had started throughout Judah. He removed the pagan idols from the land of Judah and Benjamin, as well as the cities of Ephraim that he had captured. He also repaired the bronze altar at the temple. Asa assembled the people at Jerusalem. They offered sacrifices to God and renewed their covenant with Him. God gave Asa and the people of Judah peace in the land (see ch. 15).

In the thirty-sixth year of Asa's reign, Baasha, king of Israel, went up against Judah; he wanted to stop the exodus of people from Israel into Judah. Asa sought the help of Ben-Hadad of Aram. Ben-Hadad had a treaty with Israel, but Asa hoped the silver and gold from the temple and the royal treasury he sent would convince Ben-Hadad to break the treaty and form a new alliance with Judah. Ben-Hadad agreed and attacked the cities of Israel, causing Baasha to abandon his attack on Judah (see 16:1-6).

Hanani the prophet came to Asa, telling him that because he had put his trust in Ben-Hadad rather than God, Asa's reign would be marked by war from that time forward. Incensed at the prophet's words, Asa put Hanani in prison and became brutally oppressive toward some of the people (see 16:7-10).

George H. Shaddix, "Asa: Success & Failure," *Biblical Illustrator*, Spring 2003.

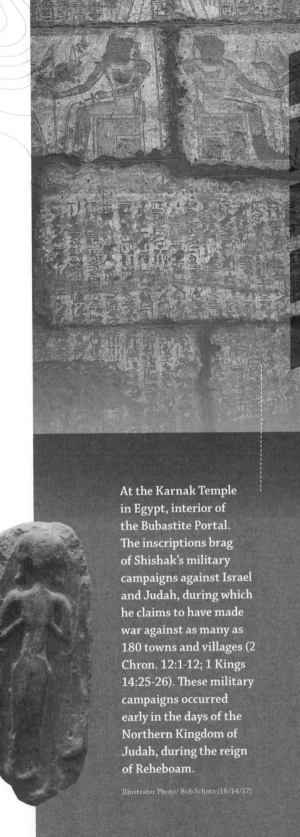

Near the end of his reign, Asa developed a severe foot disease. Even in sickness, Asa did not seek the Lord's help. He relied on physicians (see 16:12). After reigning for forty-one years, Asa died and was buried in a tomb he prepared for himself in the city of David. Jehoshaphat, the son of Asa, succeeded him as king of Judah (see 16:13-14).

A valuable lesson from the life of Asa for God's people would be the advice of Proverbs 3:5-6: "Trust in the LORD with all your heart, and do not rely on your own understanding; in all your ways know him, and he will make your paths straight."

Terra-cotta plaque from the Late Bronze Age (1550-1200 BC) depicting the Canaanite goddess Asherah; from Lachish. During his reign, Asa worked to remove all of the pagan gods from Judah.

Illustrator Photo/ British Museum/ London (31/14/16)

At the Karnak Temple in Egypt, interior of the Bubastite Portal. The inscriptions brag of Shishak's military campaigns against Israel and Judah, during which he claims to have made war against as many as 180 towns and villages (2 Chron. 12:1-12; 1 Kings 14:25-26). These military campaigns occurred early in the days of the Northern Kingdom of Judah, during the reign of Reheboam.

Illustrator Photo/ Bob Schatz (16/14/17)

Read 2 Chronicles 14:8-15.

In 2 Chronicles 13, we learn that with God's help, the army of Judah, though surrounded, was able to defeat Israel. And, in this one battle, half a million soldiers of Israel were slain. Building on this victory, Abijah (Asa's father) fortified his troops and "grew strong" (13:21). Though Abijah's reign was short, he left behind a well-organized and experienced army, but most importantly, an army that had trusted the Lord and seen victory. It is worth noting that in their battle with Israel, the soldiers of Judah "cried out to the LORD" (13:14), though there is no record of Abijah crying to the Lord.

Not only did Asa inherit an army of over half a million men, but it was a well-balanced army. The 300,000 soldiers of Judah were outfitted and adept at hand-to-hand combat. The 280,000 soldiers of Benjamin were trained and equipped for attacking the foe from a distance. Their bows were a decided advantage in that they could attack an opponent before he reached them. The verse closes by indicating that all of them were "valiant warriors" (v. 8). As any general would know, what is important is not just how many soldiers you have in the fight, but how much fight you have in your soldiers.

For all of its strength and might, Asa did not ultimately trust in his army (2 Chron. 14:11). In our own lives, how does common sense and wisdom relate to trust in the Lord?

Asa prepared for battle, but before he met Zerah, he met with God. What is significant here is not just that Asa called to the Lord, but through the content of his prayer we see clearly the focus of his trust. Asa realized only God could bring victory under the circumstances.

Do you seek the Lord's help whether or not you believe you have the strength or wisdom to overcome in a situation, or are you more likely to only seek the Lord when you feel inadequate and not up for the task? What insight does Asa's prayer give into how we are to pray?

Asa called upon the Lord as the one who could help the powerless against the mighty. Interestingly, the literal Hebrew reads, "It is not with you to help between the great and him that has no strength." The meaning is that the strong as well as the weak need the Lord's assistance to gain victory. In this situation the appeal is to the Lord to help the weak.

As a result of their trust in God, Asa and the armies of Judah saw a total victory. The text indicates that the Lord did something initially that caused the Cushite army to flee. Asa and the troops were able to follow and defeat them, bringing back much "plunder" or spoils from the battle. The lesson is obvious: When we are dependent on the Lord, we can count on His strong support.

What "fight" are you in right now? How are you asking God to move in that situation?

Read 2 Chronicles 15:1-19.

With many of the kings of Israel and Judah, their victories made them proud and often led them to trust themselves instead of the Lord. Perhaps Asa, too, was tempted in such a way after his victory, and he might have fallen to this temptation had it not been for a divine visitor. The Lord followed up the battle by sending the prophet Azariah to Asa with a message of encouragement and direction. Unlike his father Abijah, Asa didn't rest on his laurels after the victory, nor did he try to take credit for what God did. As a result of his faith and obedience, the Lord blessed him with an even greater task than protecting Judah from without. The Lord called Asa to purify Judah from within.

Notice it is the Lord who takes the initiative. The Spirit came on Azariah and sent him to Asa. The lesson to Asa in the message, and to us as well, is that the Lord is with you when you are with Him. The prophet reminded Asa and the people of their recent history. The nation suffered because they did not seek the Lord or give Him their hearts. God wanted to be sure everyone understood why He allowed them to defeat the Cushites.

How does understanding the consequences of our choices, both good and bad, help us make better choices?

Asa immediately did two things in response to Azariah's prophecy. First, he removed "the abhorrent idols from the whole land of Judah and Benjamin and from the cities he had captured in the hill country of Ephraim." The little phrase, "took courage" suggests that this was something he had already been thinking about, but was afraid to do. Secondly, Asa restored (renovated) the altar of the Lord. Both are significant.

When we set out to tear down the idols in our lives, we need to be careful that we don't simply replace them with other idols. It is all too easy to get rid of the bad things in our lives and replace them with seemingly good things. But if our focus is on anything but God Himself—even serving Him—we are idolatrous. God wants us to turn away from sin and turn toward Him, the only true Victor over sin.

Is there anything taking first place in your life besides God? How might a trusted friend answer that question about you?

Asa gathered together all Judah and Benjamin (the two tribes of the Southern Kingdom known as Judah), as well as people from three of the tribes of the Northern Kingdom (Israel). The explanation given here is significant: "They had defected to him from Israel in great numbers when they saw that the Lord his God was with him." Asa sealed this new era of following God with a special sacrifice of seven hundred oxen and seven thousand sheep from the spoils of the battle. And together with the people they made a covenant with God to seek Him with all their hearts and souls. Asa's example was followed by the people, and a great revival and time of peace resulted.

In his pursuit of holy obedience, Asa also removed Maacah from the position of queen mother because of the terrible idol she built and worshiped. Asa's actions showed his wholehearted devotion to the Lord as the preeminent authority in his life, especially since honoring family elders was almost demanded. Not only did he demote the queen mother, but he personally cut down her horrible idol, broke it into pieces, and then burned it. Verse 17 tells us that the high places were not removed from Israel, indicating that as wonderful as this revival was, it didn't reunify the nation or deal with the wrong worship of Israel (the northern ten tribes who were under a different king). Even so, in Asa we see a breath of fresh air as the wind of the Spirit blew through Judah and rekindled the flame of faith.

Asa did a difficult thing in removing his grandmother. What difficult thing is God calling you to do in order to follow and trust Him?

Read 2 Chronicles 16:1-14.

Asa was a godly king, and for the early part of his reign, he led the people as no one had since David. Unfortunately, he didn't finish as he started. In the thirty-sixth year of Asa's reign, his devotion and trust was again tested, and this time he didn't fare well.

Why is it especially sad when someone who has followed God suddenly turns away from Him and faces disastrous results?

Baasha, the wicked king of the northern ten tribes of Israel, took over Ramah, a city that served as a gateway between the two kingdoms. Most likely, Baasha tried to stem the tide of defections from Israel to Judah that Asa's good and godly reign had produced. Since the high road to and from Jerusalem passed through Ramah, he made this frontier town a military station in order to keep anyone from leaving or coming to King Asa."

Asa, instead of seeking the Lord or trusting Him to deliver, made a hasty, ill-advised treaty with the pagan king of Aram, Ben-hadad, using the temple treasures as payment. Ben-hadad accepted the payoff and attacked Israel, forcing Baasha to leave Ramah to defend his territories. In the short run, Asa's plan appeared successful.

Because of Asa's military success against Zerah the Cushite, why do you suppose Asa did not seek the Lord as he had years earlier? What might have changed in Asa's life that he would not seek God during this crisis?

Hanani was a "seer" (one who had visions from God) and was sent by the Lord to rebuke Asa. His message was a simple one: "Because you depended on the king of Aram and have not depended on the Lord your God, the army of the king of Aram has escaped from you." He reminded Asa of the victory God gave early in his reign, because "you depended on the LORD." The implication was that if Asa had trusted the Lord, God would have delivered both Baasha and Ben-hadad into his hands and two of his enemies would be gone. Now, instead of removing Ben-hadad as an enemy, Asa had strengthened him with the wealth of Judah—a mistake that would come back to haunt him. Hanani closed his rebuke with a powerful reminder of God's heart toward His people: "The eyes of the LORD roam throughout the earth to show himself strong for those who are wholeheartedly devoted to him." What a powerful promise this is! And yet, for Asa it was a haunting reminder of why he had missed a blessing. His heart was no longer completely the Lord's.

Instead of receiving this rebuke from God with a humble, penitent heart, Asa became angry and threw this messenger of the Lord into prison. God alone knows what the outcome would have been if Asa had repented in humility and asked the Lord's forgiveness. Instead, he bowed his back and refused to be instructed.

Sin always has consequences, but it seems that the greatest consequences in our lives are not for acts of sin, but for the failure to repent when we are directly confronted by the Lord with our sin. That was certainly the case with Asa.

When God confronts us with sin, His intent is that we quickly repent and turn back to Him. The wonderful news, thanks to the gospel of Jesus Christ, is that He is ready to welcome us back when we do.

Second Chronicles 15:19 may be the key verse in determining what caused King Asa to make terrible decisions in chapter 16. Based on the information in this verse, what connection might there be from the King Asa of chapters 14 and 15 to the King Asa of chapter 16 who made such ungodly choices?

HEZEKIAH

Judah's Praying King

INTRODUCTION

In times of trouble, is prayer usually your first instinct or last resort?

No matter who you are, where you live, what your economic status is, or what your religious life is like, trouble and troublemakers will find you. A Christian's response in the face of such realities may tend toward panicking or devising a plot to make things better. Sadly, the last course many of us choose is prayer.

Rather than panicking, plotting, or using persuasion, the Bible urges prayer in times of trouble. In fact, prayer should be our first response, not our last resort. A wonderful portion of Scripture that drives this point home is 2 Kings 18–19, which concerns a man named Hezekiah. His story reveals that prayer does what no plotting or persuasiveness can do.

Hezekiah began his reign as king of Judah during the third year of King Hoshea, the last king of Israel. In the fourteenth year of Hezekiah's reign, the Assyrian King Sennacherib began his military campaign into the Southern Kingdom. This included a siege against Jerusalem. Unlike the kings of the Northern Kingdom, however, Hezekiah trusted in the Lord God. Not one of the kings of Judah—either before or after his time—was like him. He did what was right in the Lord's sight just as his ancestor David. Hezekiah knew his hope for the future rested ultimately on the Lord and His saving power. This king relied on the Lord for help.

When faced with opposition, why do we often turn to human means before we place our trust in God?

Watch the video teaching for Session 5 to discover "The World of King Hezekiah," then continue the group discussion.

Focus Attention

If someone or something seemed determined to harm you or someone you love, to whom or what would you turn for help? Why?

Explore The Text

As a group, read 2 Kings 18:28-32.

Suppose you were a Hebrew standing on the wall. How would you feel after hearing Rabshakeh's words?

What "Rabshakeh" have you encountered in your life, someone who has tried to discourage you and tempt you to give up your trust in the Lord to rescue you? How do you respond to this type of objector?

As a group, read 2 Kings 19:1-7.

What was Hezekiah's first response when he heard what Rabshakeh had said (vv. 1-2)? What did this response say about his character and relationship with the Lord?

As a group, read 2 Kings 19:14-19.

What did Hezekiah do with the threatening letter from Sennacherib? Why did he do this?

When have you figuratively or literally "spread . . . out before the Lord" something that was threatening you? What happened? How did this help?

How did Hezekiah begin his prayer? Do you think this is important? Why or why not?

What reason did Hezekiah give for God to save His people? How should this impact your own prayers?

APPLY THE TEXT

The psalmist affirms, "The LORD has heard my plea for help; the LORD accepts my prayer" (Ps. 6:9). The Lord can accomplish infinitely more than we would ever dare to ask or hope. His mighty power is at work within us. What an incredible thought! The God who created the universe loves us. He cares for us. He fights our battles while we keep silent. Nothing is impossible for Him. Whatever seemingly hopeless situation we find ourselves in, God can rescue us. May He be who we turn to first in such moments, not last.

What is one situation in your life that has seemed so hopeless that you have stopped praying about it?

What are some specific ways the story of Hezekiah should influence your prayer life?

How can our group support you in prayer this week?

Close your group time in prayer, reflecting on what you have discussed.

HEZEKIAH

KEY VERSES

Then Hezekiah turned his face to the wall and prayed to the LORD, "Please, LORD, remember how I have walked before you faithfully and wholeheartedly and have done what pleases you."

— 2 Kings 20:2-3a

BASIC FACTS

1. Son and successor of Judah's King Ahaz; his mother's name was *Abi* (or Abijah).

2. Name *Hezekiah* means "Yahweh (the Lord) is my strength."

3. Became king at age twenty five; ruled in Jerusalem for twenty-nine years.

4. Lived during the time of Isaiah's prophetic ministry and the height of the Assyrian Empire.

5. Became critically ill at age thirty nine; told by Isaiah to prepare to die, but prayed for deliverance and lived fifteen extra years.

6. Died at age fifty four; buried alongside his ancestors in Jerusalem.

TIMELINE

900–850 BC

- First temple reform under Asa 897
- Omri (Israel) makes Samaria his capital 880
- Ahab reigns in Northern Kingdom 874–853
- Jehoshaphat rules in Judah 872–848
- Elijah's prophetic ministry 862–852
- Shalmaneser III becomes king in Assyria 859
- Ben-hadad (Syria) attacks Samaria 857

850–800 BC

- Elisha's prophetic ministry 850–798
- Athaliah's reign of terror in Judah 841–835
- Jehu's reign in Northern Kingdom 841–814
- Joel's prophetic ministry (early date) 836–796
- Second temple reform under Joash 812

KNOWN FOR

1. On becoming king after his wicked father's death, Hezekiah instituted spiritual reforms in Judah, including the removal of idolatrous shrines in the Jerusalem temple and on high places throughout the land. He also renewed temple worship, particularly the Passover celebration (2 Chron. 29–31).

2. In 701 BC, Hezekiah refused to pay tribute to the Assyrian Empire and faced an attack on the city of Jerusalem. Isaiah counseled the king to trust in the Lord's protection, which the Lord delivered by miraculously striking down 185,000 Assyrian warriors (2 Kings 18–19).

3. To secure water in the city during attacks, Hezekiah commissioned the digging of a 1,750-foot tunnel in the bedrock underneath Jerusalem. The fresh-water Gihon Spring flows through the tunnel into the Pool of Siloam (2 Chron. 32:2-4,30).

4. Hezekiah became deathly ill and was told by the prophet Isaiah to put his house in order. Hezekiah repented and prayed for mercy, and the Lord gave the king a miraculous sign that he would recover and live fifteen additional years: the sun's shadow moved back ten steps (2 Kings 20:1-11).

5. Hezekiah proudly showed off all of his "whole treasure house" to envoys from the rising kingdom of Babylon. Isaiah prophesied that Hezekiah's foolish action pointed to a time when Babylon would ransack Jerusalem and take the king's descendants into captivity (1 Kings 20:12-19).

800–750 BC

- Uzziah reigns in Judah 794–740
- First Olympic Games held in Greece 776
- Jonah's prophetic ministry 770
- First documented solar eclipse in Assyria 763

750–700 BC

- Isaiah's prophetic ministry 742–700
- Tiglath-pileser III rules in Assyria 745–727
- Syro-Ephraimite war against Judah 735
- Northern Kingdom conquered by Assyria 722
- Hezekiah rules in Judah 715–686
- Sennacherib (Assyria) invades Judah 701

Judah's King Hezekiah

By Gary Hardin

Hezekiah came to the throne of Judah at age twenty five (see 2 Kings 18:2) and reigned for twenty-nine years (715–686 BC). Hezekiah "did what was right in the LORD's sight" (v. 3). Hezekiah's early actions could certainly be described in terms of spiritual renewal and reforms (see v. 4). Among his reforms, he reorganized the priests and Levites and had the temple repaired and reconsecrated (see 2 Chron. 29). Hezekiah reinstated sacrificial offerings (see 29:20-24,31) and celebrated the Passover (see 30:2-3). Hezekiah was persistent in establishing these reforms, and God rewarded him (see 31:20-21).

In 701 BC, Assyria's King Sennacherib led his army southward toward Judah, conquering many fortified cities along the way. In preparation, Hezekiah diverted and secured Jerusalem's water supplies, repaired and fortified the city walls, and built towers on the wall (see 2 Chron. 32:1-8). Before Sennacherib's army arrived at Jerusalem, Hezekiah attempted to make peace. He took all the gold and silver in his treasury and stripped the gold and silver from the temple and gave it to Sennacherib (see Kings 18:13-16). The attempt failed. Even pious Hezekiah showed a lapse of faith and trust in God.

Sennacherib sent "a massive army" to besiege Jerusalem (2 Kings 18:17). Assyria's royal spokesman mocked God and warned that Jerusalem would be destroyed if Hezekiah did not make some kind of bargain with him (vv. 19-25).

Hezekiah took his concerns about this crisis to God in prayer (see Isa. 37:14-20). The prophet Isaiah responded with a prophecy of Sennacherib's fall (see vv. 21-35). Scripture records the fulfillment of Isaiah's prophecy (see 2 Kings 19:35-36; Isa. 37:36-37).

Sometime prior to 701 BC, a serious illness struck Hezekiah. Isaiah told him to prepare for his death (Isa. 38:1). King Hezekiah prayed for additional years of life, and God promised him fifteen more (vv. 2-6). God gave Hezekiah a sign that he would be healed. A shadow cast by the sun moved backward from its normal direction (vv. 7-8). Hezekiah had received a promise of recovery, but also the promise that God would deliver Jerusalem from the Assyrians (vv. 5-6).

Later an envoy from Babylon urged Hezekiah to form an alliance with Babylon in order to protect Judah. When this group lavished gifts upon Hezekiah, he, in turn, showed

Gary Hardin, "Judah's King Hezekiah," *Biblical Illustrator*, Fall 2018

them his wealth—an action that brought both a stiff rebuke from Isaiah and a warning about the coming Babylonian captivity (Isa. 39:1-7). This event highlights two of Hezekiah's weaknesses: his vulnerability to flattery and his pride about his possessions.

Hezekiah enjoyed the extension of his life. Likely during this time he encouraged literary efforts in Judah, which included copying some of Solomon's proverbs. The later part of Hezekiah's reign was uneventful, except for some building projects around Jerusalem (see 2 Kings 20:20; 2 Chron. 32:27-32). Hezekiah died in 686 BC. His son, Manasseh, succeeded him (2 Kings 20:21).

At the bottom of these steps is the Gihon Spring in the Kidron Valley. King Hezekiah had a tunnel dug from the spring to the Pool of Siloam; he did this to provide a water supply for Jerusalem that would be accessible from inside the city walls and thus inaccessible to attackers.

Illustrator Photo/ Bob Schatz (9/38/5)

Read 2 Kings 18:1-8.

Judah was in dire straits when Hezekiah, the "Strength of Jehovah," ascended the throne at the age of twenty five after the death of his father in 728 BC. The political situation was particularly humiliating. The financial tribute paid to the pagan nation, Assyria, by former King Ahaz, was expected to continue. The leaders of Israel were in favor of the continued tribute, because it served to protect Israel, and it gave them a bond of union with Assyria's "Great King," which in essence made the Israelites slaves.

Members of the royal family and nobility administered justice, encroaching on the power of the king, and the common citizens lived in fear of them. The priests were largely corrupt, and most of the prophets abused their office to selfish and dishonorable ends. Indifferent to the result, they gave mock revelations to the people as their patrons directed, and too often led the masses astray. The true prophets, faithful to their duty, were public enemies, while their rivals were held up as patriots.

When have you recently witnessed or experienced injustice? Do you see it growing more or less prevalent today? Explain.

The public turned against the faithful, and the servants of God had to hide for their lives. The majority of the people were impoverished, the rich were selfish and oppressive, the judges corrupt, and heathen superstition invaded every level of society. The government was torn by rival factions. One party urged a treaty with Egypt; another the continuance of the Assyrian tribute; and a third stood up for national independence. Hezekiah had no light task before him to guide public affairs, and he was only twenty-five!

What made the task of uniting the people much more difficult for a king like Hezekiah? What kinds of skills would he need in order to be successful?

As king, Hezekiah was inclined to seek peaceful means of resolution rather than violence. Though he could wrestle cities from the Philistines and defend Jerusalem in war, he gave his heart to the promotion of the internal welfare of his kingdom. Fond of agriculture and pastoral pursuits, like his grandfather Uzziah, Hezekiah had great herds and flocks in the Negeb and elsewhere, and he built shepherds' towers and large folds for their protection.

Vineyards, olive yards, and cornfields were Hezekiah's delight. His tender religious sensibility and poetic genius—the first instance of the latter since King David—are seen in the hymn he composed after his recovery from almost mortal sickness. His love of culture displayed itself in his zeal for the preservation of the religious writings of his nation, of which their literature to a great extent consisted. Descended, apparently on his mother's side, from Zechariah, the favorite prophet of Uzziah, Hezekiah inherited a lofty enthusiasm for the ancient faith. In direct contrast to his father, who had zealously favored everything Assyrian, Hezekiah gave himself passionately to whatever was national, and devoted his life to the restoration of the worship of Jehovah and the purification of the land from the heathenism which Ahaz had introduced.

How might Hezekiah's love for his nation, and a passion to see God worshiped and pagan influences removed, set the stage for the people to return to God in their hearts and lives?

Have you turned from God in any area of your life? In what way do you, like the people of Hezekiah's day, need to repent of any wrongdoing and seek God wholeheartedly?

Read 2 Chronicles 29.

The Law was King Hezekiah's guiding star in public as well as private. The prophets were his honored and cherished counselors. As intelligent and refined as he was humble and godly, Hezekiah took measures to collect and arrange the sacred books. He appointed a royal commission to gather the materials, which now form the Book of Proverbs. Jewish tradition also ascribes to him the collecting of the prophecies of Isaiah and the preservation of Ecclesiastes. King Ahaz had closed the gates of the temple. Hezekiah not only reopened them, but put the whole building into a time of repair, and revived the use of the psalms of David and Asaph in public worship.

Each person played his or her part in this large, communal honoring of God. They worshiped God with the best words they could find—the words of the great psalms of praise written by David and others.

Once they had properly sacrificed and cleansed the temple and their own hearts before the Lord, the assembly was invited to come and bring their personal offerings. One of the great purposes of the temple—as a place for the personal sacrifice and worship of the believer—was now restored.

If you could implement religious and political reforms in your community, where would you start?

To secure the maintenance of the priests and Levites, Hezekiah restored the payment of the tithes fixed by the Law of Moses, including "the best of the grain, new wine, fresh oil, honey, and of all the produce of the field, and they brought in an abundance, a tenth of everything" (2 Chron. 31:5). Without oppressing the people, his wise and upright rule kept his treasury always full, and his palace boasted of stores of spices and costly oil, and a well-appointed armory. Jewish tradition fancied that he must have been the promised Messiah; and 2 Kings reflects upon him like this: "Hezekiah relied on the Lord God of Israel; not one of the kings of Judah was like him, either before him or after him" (2 Kings 18:5).

When you think of great leaders from the past who have brought about change and reform, who comes to mind?

Who in your life has proven to be an inspiration to you? How?

When was the last time that a message from God caught your attention? What was it? What did you do?

Read 2 Kings 18:9-12 and 2 Chronicles 30.

The northern kingdom of Israel had come to ruin. Though there had been animosity between Israel and the people of Judah (the Southern Kingdom) where King Hezekiah reigned, it was gone. Most of the people of Israel had been taken away to Assyria as prisoners, and only a remnant of their population remained.

Messengers from King Hezekiah were sent through the whole land, inviting all to come to the Passover at Jerusalem. Unfortunately, their invitation was largely rejected as the people left in the north had finally lapsed into heathenism. Some, however, were still found in Manasseh, Asher, and Zebulon, who honored the God of their fathers, and gladly accepted the summons.

What factors might contribute to a person declining an invitation to worship and fellowship with others?

Preparations had to be made for such a gathering. Because he was strict in his obedience to the Mosaic law, Hezekiah caused Jerusalem to be thoroughly purified. The idolatrous altars raised by Ahaz were destroyed, and their material thrown into the Kidron Valley. Enthusiasm began to spread through the whole community.

Priests and Levites who had neglected to complete their ceremonial cleansing were roused to do so. As in former times, household fathers and Levites sacrificed the lambs for their families. Perhaps because of the idolatry in their land, many of the visitors from the north failed to comply with the ceremonial demands of the day, but Hezekiah declared they should join in the feast as well. He prayed for them, lest they should suffer as threatened in Leviticus, for neglect of the commandments of the Law.

Is it necessary to "clean up" prior to worshiping God? Should people come as they are? Explain.

Then came the great celebration and along with it chants, music, sacrifices, and general gladness, as happened in the dedication of the temple by Solomon. Seven days, the legal duration, was not long enough for such a jubilee; the feast was prolonged for seven more days. For two weeks, the people of the Northern and Southern Kingdoms worshiped and celebrated their God, all at the initiation of Hezekiah.

Why were the people so enthusiastic to join in the worship and celebration of God? Do we see this today? Why or why not?

Hezekiah did all he could to make the revival of faith permanent. In the middle of it all, Isaiah and other prophets were zealously proclaiming spiritual truth. Prominent in their messages was a vision of the future. The nation ever more began to anticipate the Messiah, God's deliverer who would restore peace, order, and Israel's place among the nations.

Have you ever found yourself thinking about the return of Christ? What questions do you have?

By the time Jesus was born, the people of Israel fully anticipated an imminent appearance of the Messiah. Jesus was the Messiah, but the people didn't acknowledge Him as such. Why do people today continue to reject Jesus as the Messiah?

JOSIAH

Israel's Good King

INTRODUCTION

To what degree do the previous generations impact our own?

The story of Josiah is a testimony to the Lord's ability to work in and through those who acknowledge Him as the one true God, even if their parents and grandparents before them did not. Josiah's life is set before us as an example of the dynamic impact the choice to follow God can make.

Josiah was born in 648 BC to the family of a young sixteen-year-old Amon, son of Manasseh, king of Judah. Amon was both young and wicked. He died eight years later, after reigning two years as king; and his son Josiah became king at the age of eight. In a land saturated with the influences of idolatry, Josiah stands as one who chose to seek the Lord as David had—to follow the Lord and His Word fully, regardless of what others did. In the Scriptural account of the life of Josiah, we find many others who were willing to follow God in the midst of a society that followed its own desires. We can learn many lessons from the life, times, and choices of Josiah, lessons that will serve us well in a time much like his.

Who has had the biggest influence on your life?

Who comes to mind as someone that you have significantly influenced?

Watch the video teaching for Session 6 to discover "The World of King Josiah," then continue the group discussion.

FOCUS ATTENTION

What kind of spiritual legacy did you grow up in? How did it affect your own faith?

EXPLORE THE TEXT

As a group, read 2 Kings 21:19-24.

What characterized the reign of Amon, Josiah's father?

What might it have been like to grow up as a young boy under such a father? How might Amon's beliefs and choices have impacted young Josiah?

As a group, read 2 Kings 22:1-7.

It is uncommon for the names of mothers to be mentioned when a kingly lineage is shared. Why might the author have put Josiah's mother's name in his story?

Josiah was blessed with the companionship of those who wanted what was right. They were loyal to Josiah and doubtless had an impact for godliness in the young child's life. What kind of influence do you think these men had on the young King Josiah?

What benefits might have been associated with beginning religious reforms in the temple, as opposed to all the other places reform was needed in the land?

As a group, read 2 Kings 22:8-13.

Why did Josiah respond so strongly to what he read in the newly found Book of the Law? Was his reaction justified? Explain.

Apply The Text

What an incredible thing it is to think of Josiah taking the throne of Judah at the age of eight. What an awesome responsibility placed on such small shoulders! Yet in retrospect, he turns out to be one of the greatest kings Judah ever had. Many things wove together to shape the man he would become. Certainly he was impacted by the repentance of his grandfather, Manasseh. Even apart from his personal memories would be the constant reminders from the people of the change in this initially wicked king. We can assume that another major influence was the prophet Zephaniah, whose ministry began a year before Josiah took the throne and continued until he was about seventeen years old. Zephaniah's message of soon-coming judgment from the Lord may have been the catalyst for a turning point in Josiah at age sixteen, when we are told that he "began to seek the God of his ancestor David" (2 Chron. 34:3). Another turning point in his life is recorded as being the twelfth year of his reign (when he was about twenty years old), when he began purging Judah and Jerusalem of idols and wrong worship. It may be that Jeremiah, whose ministry began about this time, was an influencer in Josiah's zeal.

What are some of the marks of Josiah's faith that are most meaningful to you?

How could you be a bigger influence in the life of someone who is young in his or her faith?

Who has had the most positive influence on your spiritual life so far? Call or write this person a note to show appreciation for his or her influence on you.

Close your group time in prayer, reflecting on what you have discussed.

JOSIAH

KEY VERSE

Before him there was no king like him who turned to the LORD with all his heart and with all his soul and with all his strength according to all the law of Moses, and no one like him arose after him.

— 2 Kings 23:25

BASIC FACTS

1. Grandson of Manasseh and son of King Amon and Jedidah. He became Judah's fifteenth king.

2. Name *Josiah* means "Yahweh (the Lord) is my healing [or support]."

3. Became king of Judah at age eight when his father was assassinated after only two years as ruler.

4. Had a spiritual experience of renewal at age 16 that led to radical reforms throughout Judah.

5. Reigned 31 years until his death in battle at Megiddo in 609 BC.

TIMELINE

800–750 BC

- Uzziah reigns in Judah 794–740
- First Olympic Games held in Greece 776
- Jonah's prophetic ministry 770
- First documented solar eclipse in Assyria 763
- City of Rome founded 753

750–700 BC

- Isaiah's prophetic ministry 742–700
- Tiglath-pileser III rules in Assyria 745–727
- Syro-Ephraimite war against Judah 735
- Northern Kingdom conquered by Assyria 722
- Hezekiah rules in Judah 715–686
- Third temple reform under Hezekiah 715
- Sennacherib (Assyria) invades Judah 701

KNOWN FOR

1. Josiah's grandfather became king at age twelve and reigned fifty-five years; his father inherited the throne at age twenty two and served two years before being assassinated. Both kings were idolatrous and wicked, contrasting sharply with Josiah's faithfulness to the Lord from his youth until his death.

2. In the eighteenth year of Josiah's reign, the king ordered the repair of the temple. In the process, the book of the Law was found and read to the king. In response, Josiah initiated a covenant renewal service in the temple at which he and the people pledged themselves to follow the Lord and keep His commands (2 Kings 22:3-13; 23:1-3).

3. Following the covenant renewal service, Josiah instituted a wide-ranging set of reforms that included purging the land of idols and pagan altars. He destroyed an altar to the false god Molech—where child sacrifice was practiced—in the Hinnom Valley outside of Jerusalem, and executed the priests who served at all the idolatrous shrines (2 Kings 23:4-20).

4. Josiah reinstated the observance of the Passover in Jerusalem, which by some accounts had not been observed in the city for more than four centuries—since the time of the judges (2 Kings 23:21-23; 2 Chron. 35:1-19).

5. Josiah's reign ended when he led his army to the Valley of Megiddo to prevent the Egyptian pharaoh's troops from joining an alliance with the Assyrians against the Babylonians. Josiah was struck by arrows while riding in his war chariot and later died of those wounds (2 Kings 23:28-30; 2 Chron. 35:20-24).

700–600 BC

- Sennacherib destroys city of Babylon 689
- His son, Esarhaddon, rebuilds Babylon 676
- Josiah reigns in Judah 640–609
- Josiah enacts reforms; finds the Law 631–622
- Jeremiah's prophetic ministry 627–585
- Assyrian Empire ends with fall of Nineveh 612
- Daniel and friends taken to Babylon 605

600–500 BC

- Nebuchadnezzar takes Jehoiachin captive 597
- Ezekiel's prophetic ministry 593–570
- Jerusalem destroyed; people captured 586
- Temple of Solomon looted and burned 586
- Cyrus of Persia takes Babylon 539
- Edict of Cyrus allows Jews to return 539
- Second temple completed 515

Josiah: His Rule and Reforms

By Kevin C. Peacock

King Josiah ruled Judah from 640–609 BC. Josiah came to the throne when he was eight years old (2 Chron. 34:1). At sixteen, he began his personal faith journey with Israel's God; at the age of twenty, he began to purge the land of its paganism (v. 3).

Josiah's Reforms—Second Chronicles 34–35 detail five aspects of Josiah's reforms. First, Josiah removed the religious apostasy of his father Amon and grandfather Manasseh (34:4-7). Second, he instigated the repair of the temple in Jerusalem, which was undertaken by the Levites (34:8-13).

Third, during the repair of the temple, Hilkiah the priest discovered a Torah scroll (34:14-28). Upon hearing the Torah scroll being read, Josiah responded humbly and penitently by tearing his clothes as a sign of mourning. He recognized the importance of the document and sent it to be authenticated by Huldah the prophetess (34:20-21). Huldah delivered a two-fold message: an oracle of punishment on Jerusalem and Judah based on the curses of Deuteronomy 28 (34:23-25), and an oracle of salvation for Josiah based on his humility before God's Word (34:26-28). Josiah would die "in peace" in the sense that his eyes would not see the disaster that God would bring on Jerusalem and its inhabitants.

Fourth, after the Torah scroll discovery, Josiah led the people in covenant renewal (34:29-33). Josiah imposed a pledge of obedience on the assembly. The people, however, did not share Josiah's personal faith, as borne out by the sad fact that Josiah's religious reforms died when he died (36:14-16).

Josiah's reforms culminated in the Passover celebration (35:1-19). The Passover unified Israel. The king, the priests, the Levites, and all the people together celebrated the meal and reclaimed their history and the foundations of Israel as a community.

Josiah's Death—In 609 BC, Pharaoh Neco II traveled northward to help the Assyrian forces as they fought against the Babylonians. Josiah attempted to prevent Neco from traveling through his territory at Megiddo. Neco warned Josiah that he was following God's orders, and that God Himself might destroy Josiah if he interfered. But Josiah did not heed Neco's warning and died in battle (35:20-24).

Josiah's Legacy—Josiah removed all traces of foreign worship from the land and consolidated Hebrew worship to Jerusalem. However, not even Josiah's

Kevin C. Peacock, "Josiah: His Rule and Reforms," *Biblical Illustrator*, Fall 2019.

A Torah scroll,
from Jerusalem.

Illustrator Photo/ Bob Svhatz/ Royal
Ontario Museum,/ Toronto (29/16/6)

sweeping reforms could cool Yahweh's wrath over Manasseh's outrageous reign (2 Kings 23:26-27). Judah fell to the Babylonians in 586 BC, and most of the Jewish leadership was taken to Babylon (2 Chron. 36:17-21). Josiah's godliness could preserve neither him from his premature death nor his nation from the upcoming exile (34:24-25). The biblical writer remembered Josiah as Judah's greatest king, "Before him there was no king like him who turned to the Lord with all his heart and with all his soul and with all his strength according to all the law of Moses, and no one like him arose after him" (2 Kings 23:25).

Looking out of the gate at Megiddo with a view of the surrounding plain.
Judah's King Josiah was killed at the Battle of Megiddo in 609 BC.

Illustrator Photo/ G.B. Howell (35/63/59)

Read 2 Chronicles 34:1-8.

Josiah grew up with a father and grandfather who did not follow God (although his grandfather, Manasseh, did repent and led spiritual reforms that were supposed to draw the nation back to God).

Who in your family has had the greatest positive impact on your spiritual growth and development? Why do you say that?

"In the eighth year of his reign," Josiah would have been sixteen (he became king at age eight). He was still a young man and had not undertaken public duties. He probably was under the control and direction of a regent. However, in matters of personal religion he displayed personal piety. When he was twenty one, he began his active reforms in Judah and Jerusalem, which he purged of high places, Asherah poles, carved idols, and images.

Josiah was determined to complete the work of uprooting the apostasy of his grandfather Manasseh's reign. Ultimately, he was unable to free the people of their attachments to paganism. It is in this sense that kings rightly attribute the decline and fall of Judah to Manasseh's reign. Notwithstanding Manasseh's later repentance, neither Josiah nor anyone else was able to pull back the forces Manasseh had released early in his career.

Verses 4-5 take up further details of Josiah's reform (compare v. 4b with 2 Kings 23:6; and v. 5a with 2 Kings 23:14,16,20). Though not explicitly stated, it is implied that Josiah executed the priests of Baal (2 Kings 23:20) following the precedent set by Jehu (2 Kings 10) and Jehoiada (2 Chron. 23:17). The punishment is fitted to the crime: the priests who burned sacrifices to Baal had their own bones burned on the same altar. According to 2 Kings 23:16, the bones of priests who had died were removed from their graves and burned.

Why is it important to remove sin and sinful influences from our lives?

These reforming activities were carried north to Manasseh, Ephraim, and Simeon, as far as Naphtali. The appearance of Simeon here is unexpected. That tribe was normally located to the south of Judah (1 Chron. 4:24-33). Meanwhile, Nineveh was besieged by Cyaxares and the Medes in 625 BC. The Babylonians had broken free, and tribes from the north were raiding former Assyrian lands. It was a golden opportunity for Josiah to extend his control into Israel, even as far as Upper Galilee (Naphtali).

What do you find surprising about Josiah's reforms?

This passage of Scripture shows several important things to the reader. First, Josiah was a very young man, yet he had a spiritual maturity and depth that was not found in his father and grandfather. He was convicted that the right thing to do was follow God and worship Him only. His list of reform actions is long and extensive indeed. Sin had become so commonplace that it took massive reform to get the people to remove the pagan worship places and practices instituted by Josiah's father and grandfather.

If you've come from a home where Christ was not served and honored, you can be just like Josiah and make a break with that lifestyle that doesn't satisfy. Josiah broke the cycle in his family, and you can too.

Read 2 Chronicles 34:14-21.

In the process of cleaning and repairing the temple, Hilkiah the high priest found a copy of the Book of the Law (2 Chron. 34:14). It's possible it had been hidden by a priest to protect it from destruction by one of the wicked kings such as Manasseh (Josiah's grandfather) or Amon (Josiah's father). Perhaps it had been removed when the ark was removed from the Holy of Holies by one of these kings. Many believe this scroll contained the entire Pentateuch (Genesis, Exodus, Leviticus, Numbers, Deuteronomy), while others believe it was a copy of Deuteronomy.

Hilkiah gave the scroll to Shaphan who took it immediately to King Josiah (2 Chron. 34:15-18). He read the Book of the Law to the king, and Josiah was struck by the seriousness of being in a covenant relationship with the Lord God of Israel. Josiah realized that Judah was due the wrath of God for their unfaithfulness.

What did Josiah do when he heard the reading of the Book of the Law? What do you see about his attitude toward the Word of God?

Josiah tore his robes in anguish over the evident sin of the people of Judah. His first action was to send his most trusted men to inquire of the Lord for him and for those in Israel and Judah. He wanted to know what the Lord would say at this time in the life of the nation. Josiah knew the absolute necessity of obeying the Word of God, and he was seeking to do that with all his heart.

The men went to Huldah, a prophetess who lived in a section of Jerusalem on the west side, probably built under Hezekiah's leadership. Huldah faithfully spoke the message God had for Josiah and the people of the land.

Read 2 Kings 22:15-17. What was God's message to the people of Judah? Why was this going to happen (v. 17)?

The message was clear: Because they had forsaken the Lord and followed other gods, the Lord's wrath was already kindled against them, and it would certainly come upon them and not be quenched. God warned them, and now He fulfilled His Word. Judah would "become a desolation and a curse" (2 Kings 22:19).

Read 2 Kings 22:18-20. What was God's message to Josiah? Why was it different?

The message to Josiah was also a fulfillment of the Word of God. Josiah had a tender heart, sensitive to what the Lord said. When he heard the Word, he immediately humbled himself before the Lord. He wept and cried out to the Lord in prayer. Because of that, Josiah would die in peace without seeing the desolation the Lord would bring on Judah and its inhabitants.

Read 2 Kings 23:1-3. What do you see about the place of the Word of God in Josiah's thoughts and actions?

The first thing Josiah did was call the elders of Judah and Jerusalem to a meeting at the temple. The people of Judah and Jerusalem went along with him. The priests and the prophets were there as well, which probably included Zephaniah, Jeremiah, and possibly Habakkuk and Nahum. Josiah had little to say. He simply began reading the words of the book of the covenant which could have included all the first five Books of the Law. He made a personal covenant to follow the Lord and His Word. The people followed his lead and entered into that covenant. The Word of God made an impact not only on Josiah, but, under his leadership, on the nation as well.

Read 2 Chronicles 35.

In his eighteenth year as king, Josiah reinstituted the celebration of Passover. Evidently, Passover had not been observed to the magnitude that Josiah ordered it celebrated since the days of the prophet Samuel (2 Chron. 35:18). King Josiah and his officials worked diligently to make the Passover an important event again, and one in which people remembered the past and celebrated God's goodness to them.

Passover was one of Israel's most important celebrations, a commemoration of a significant event in God's deliverance of Israel from slavery to the Egyptians. God's angel passed over every home in which the family had sprinkled blood on its doorpost in obedience to God's command; but when the Lord's angel saw a home with no blood covering the doorpost, the life of the home's firstborn was taken (see Ex. 12:1-30).

Before the Passover could be observed by the people, the leaders of the people had to prepare for the celebration. King Josiah "encouraged them to serve in the LORD's temple" (2 Chron. 35:2). The religious leaders who served in the temple needed a "morale boost," because the work they were instructed to do would set the tone for the entire Passover celebration. King Josiah encouraged them to return to God's Word, and to make preparations according to the instructions given by Moses and King David.

What does preparation for an event say about the importance of the event and the guest of honor?

King Josiah and his officials took the lead in providing for the Passover celebration. Josiah reached deep into his own pockets and provided a total of thirty-thousand sheep and goats for the Passover (2 Chron. 35:7). In addition, he provided three-thousand cattle, all from his own possessions. Josiah's officials also joined in by providing generously. Scripture says that they gave generously by providing (voluntarily) much of what was needed for the people and for the Levites, the religious leaders who would be overseeing the celebration itself (2 Chron. 35:8-9).

When have you experienced joy in giving generously to the Lord's work?

How has going "above and beyond" your normal acts of generosity toward God's work brought you closer to Him? In what ways did it strengthen and deepen your relationship with Him?

King Josiah is an example of a king who broke with family tradition. Remember that his father and grandfather were evil leaders who did not honor God. Josiah became king at age eight, and in time he broke with his family's tradition of rebelling against God by leading the nation back to God, removing detestable worship practices to foreign and false gods, and returning the heart of the people back to God through things like this elaborate and meaningful worship centered around Passover.

If you have not been leading well in your household, or you have somehow led you and your family away from God, take courage from Josiah's example. Make the break and start anew. He did, and he was only a teenager when he began his reforms. Turn back to the Lord, love Him with all your heart and mind, worship Him with others, and give to His work generously.

TIPS FOR LEADING A SMALL GROUP

Follow these guidelines to prepare for each group session.

PRAYERFULLY PREPARE

Review

Review the weekly material and group questions ahead of time.

Pray

Be intentional about praying for each person in the group. Ask the Holy Spirit to work through you and the group discussion as you point to Jesus each week through God's Word.

MINIMIZE DISTRACTIONS

Create a comfortable environment. If group members are uncomfortable, they'll be distracted and therefore not engaged in the group experience. Plan ahead by considering these details:

Seating

Temperature

Lighting

Food or Drink

Surrounding Noise

General Cleanliness

At best, thoughtfulness and hospitality show guests and group members they're welcome and valued in whatever environment you choose to gather. At worst, people may never notice your effort, but they're also not distracted. Do everything in your ability to help people focus on what's most important: connecting with God, with the Bible, and with one another.

INCLUDE OTHERS

Your goal is to foster a community in which people are welcome just as they are but encouraged to grow spiritually. Always be aware of opportunities to include any people who visit the group and to invite new people to join your group. An inexpensive way to make first-time guests feel welcome or to invite someone to get involved is to give them their own copies of this Bible study book.

ENCOURAGE DISCUSSION

A good small-group experience has the following characteristics.

Everyone Participates

Encourage everyone to ask questions, share responses, or read aloud.

No One Dominates—Not Even the Leader

Be sure that your time speaking as a leader takes up less than half of your time together as a group. Politely guide discussion if anyone dominates.

Nobody Is Rushed Through Questions

Don't feel that a moment of silence is a bad thing. People often need time to think about their responses to questions they've just heard or to gain courage to share what God is stirring in their hearts.

Input Is Affirmed and Followed Up

Make sure you point out something true or helpful in a response. Don't just move on. Build community with follow-up questions, asking how other people have experienced similar things or how a truth has shaped their understanding of God and the Scripture you're studying. People are less likely to speak up if they fear that you don't actually want to hear their answers or that you're looking for only a certain answer.

God and His Word Are Central

Opinions and experiences can be helpful, but God has given us the truth. Trust God's Word to be the authority and God's Spirit to work in people's lives. You can't change anyone, but God can. Continually point people to the Word and to active steps of faith.

HOW TO USE THE LEADER GUIDE

PREPARE TO LEAD

Each session of the Leader Guide is designed to be torn out so you, the leader, can have this front-and-back page with you as you lead your group through the session. Watch the session teaching video and read through the session content with the Leader Guide tear-out in hand and notice how it supplements each section of the study.

FOCUS ATTENTION

These questions are provided to help get the discussion started. They are generally more introductory and topical in nature.

EXPLORE THE TEXT

Questions in this section have some sample answers or discussion prompts provided in the Leader Guide, if needed, to help you jump-start or steer the conversation.

APPLY THE TEXT

This section contains questions that allow group members an opportunity to apply the content they have been discussing together.

BIOGRAPHY AND FURTHER INSIGHT MOMENT

These sections aren't covered in the leader guide and may be used during the group session or by group members as a part of the personal study time during the week. If you choose to use them during your group session, make sure you are familiar with the content and how you intend to use it before your group meets.

Conclude each group session with a prayer.

SESSION 1 | LEADER GUIDE

Focus Attention

How might adding ingredients to or deleting ingredients from a recipe have disastrous results? What are the benefits of following a recipe to the letter?

- A small deviation can have disastrous results in food preparation. The same thing is true to an even greater degree when it comes to obedience to the Lord.

Explore The Text

Ask a volunteer to read 1 Samuel 13:1,5-14.

In what ways did Saul disobey God in these verses, and why was his disobedience so serious? In what ways can fear prompt people to disobey God?

- Saul offered the burnt offering (not his role or place to do so) instead of waiting on the prophet Samuel to arrive and perform the function.

- Fear can cause people to be paralyzed to the point they choose not to act on something they know God has commanded them to do.

- Fear can also cause people to respond defensively, feeling an unnecessary desire to control the situation. Some might take matters into their own hands rather than continuing to wait on God, trusting Him to act.

Do you feel that Saul's punishment was suitable to the consequences he suffered? Why or why not?

- We might be tempted to think Saul's punishment was too harsh, but this is a good opportunity to remind ourselves that partial obedience is no obedience. Further, Saul consistently displayed an unwillingness to take seriously the commands of God.

Ask a volunteer to read 1 Samuel 15:1-3.

Why did the Amalekites deserve such a severe punishment? What does this show you about God's character?

- The Amalekites took advantage of Israel as millions of them left Egypt in search of the promised land; Israel was practically defenseless and caught off guard by the swift attack.

- God is a God of justice. He sees, remembers and avenges the oppressed. Sin must be judged, and people must be held accountable for their actions.

Ask a volunteer to read 1 Samuel 15:7-15,20-23.

Yet again, Saul and his army only partially complied with the Lord's command. Why did they disobey this time? What was the Lord's reaction to this?

- Saul followed God's command to slay the Amalekites, but he did not obey completely. On the surface it appears he did a good job, but the reality is he partially obeyed God, which was tantamount to being disobedient.

- Israel kept the best of the plunder—the good things—and destroyed the weak or despised things they found. Israel couldn't see letting good things go to waste.

Saul built a monument to himself. Based on this, what did he think about himself, and what did he think about God?

- Saul must have believed that because he almost fully obeyed God's commands, that was good enough or close enough to what God wanted. Yet his "good" intentions led to partial obedience and to self-worship. Essentially, Saul held himself in higher esteem than He did the Lord.

Do you think Saul was truly surprised that his behaviors were sinful, or do you think he was attempting to redefine his disobedience as something acceptable? Explain.

- Saul failed to realize that what pleases the Lord is obedience, not the religious rituals themselves. At the same time, it may be that Saul simply used these excuses to cover up his actual convictions that what he had done wasn't wrong.

APPLY THE TEXT

Why is partial obedience to God, even substantial obedience, insufficient?

In what ways can our group encourage one another to obey God more fully in all areas of faith and life?

"To obey is better than sacrifice" (1 Sam. 15:22). In what areas are you substituting sacrifice for obedience?

SESSION 2 | LEADER GUIDE

FOCUS ATTENTION

List some qualities people look for in a person who is going to lead a nation. What is the most important quality in your mind?

- People differ on what they consider to be important qualities. Charisma, wealth, success, military training, or experience in politics are frequently prized characteristics. Often, however, God's criteria differs from our own.

EXPLORE THE TEXT

Ask a volunteer to read 1 Samuel 16:1-10.

Is God impressed by the same qualities that impress us? Why or why not?

- God's choice of David should not lead us to conclude that God cares nothing for competency or skill when it comes to serving Him. Yet God's choice of David does highlight that God delights in equipping those He has called so that He gets the glory.

Why did Samuel initially think Eliab was the Lord's choice? What's the irony here (see 1 Sam. 10:23-24)?

- Given Eliab's stature—that is, his physical appearance—Samuel initially believed him to be the one God had chosen. Ironically, Samuel was drawn to someone who resembled the physical characteristics of Saul, and the Lord used this experience to teach Samuel something important.

What does verse 7 suggest about the qualities God counts as most important for His servants?

- Our culture evaluates people by their appearance, social status, and other superficial traits. Nevertheless, people do not see what God sees. Outward appearances often deceive people, but they never deceive God.

Ask volunteer to read 1 Samuel 16:11-13.

What characteristic would seem to hinder David from being anointed as king (v. 11)?

- Jesse's assumption was that David was disqualified from consideration due to his young age, which is why he was not even present for Samuel.

What did David's faithfulness in watching the sheep say about his character? How did this prepare him for the future (see 1 Sam. 17:34-37; Ps. 23)?

- David's faithful work as a shepherd reminds us of two important truths. First, it doesn't matter what we do, but how we do it. No matter what tasks we are given, we are to do them in a way that brings glory to God. Second, we learn that God is working behind the scenes in David's life in order to prepare him for his future role as king. Tending sheep helped prepare David to rule Israel. "Shepherd" would become a symbolic job description for king. God intended for the king to care for people with the same compassion that a shepherd gives to the flock. Also, David's encounters with predators developed skills that later became useful in combat.

Reflecting on this passage as a whole, what qualified David to be king? Why did God choose David?

- While the author of 1 Samuel does note that David was healthy and handsome, these qualities are not mentioned as reasons for his qualification to be king. Ultimately, the reason David became king was because God chose him. God did not choose David because of any particular trait or skill of David's, but simply because God willed to use him for this particular time and purpose.

- Throughout the Bible, God chose unlikely people to join Him in His plans to redeem mankind from sin. You may not think of yourself as a likely candidate to lead anything of a spiritual nature. Perhaps you've even said no to opportunities to provide needed leadership at your church. But the Bible is full of people with less than perfect backgrounds. It seems that these are the kinds of people God chooses—broken, imperfect, yet full of promise when they seek forgiveness, strive to do God's will, repent of past mistakes, and move on in the grace only God can provide.

APPLY THE TEXT

Who do you identify with most in this story—Samuel, Jesse, Jesse's sons, or David? Why?

How might knowing that God has chosen you to serve Him change the way that you view your occupation or role in life?

SESSION 3 | LEADER GUIDE

Focus Attention

Where do people turn to get wisdom today? Why might these sources of human wisdom fall short and disappoint the person asking for help?

- People are not perfect. While they have some wisdom to share, the wisdom of humans is no match for the wisdom God possesses, wisdom He freely gives to those who seek Him (see Jas. 1:5).

Explore The Text

Ask a volunteer to read 1 Kings 3:1-9.

How do you suppose you would respond to God if He said to you, "Ask. What should I give you?" Explain.

- God saw Solomon's heart to serve and worship Him, and He asked Solomon to name a gift that he wanted to receive from the Lord.

- One might expect many to respond with "riches" or "fame" or "long life." The request would typically center around the needs of the person being asked the question.

Why did Solomon desire wisdom above anything else? What does this reveal about him and his relationship with God?

- Solomon acknowledged that God was the cause of his rise to power. In contrast to his own personal and experiential lack of stature, Solomon had to lead a people whose greatness was first measured by the fact that they were chosen by God. Solomon needed to embody God's standards for the people. With all of their growth under his father David, Solomon likely sensed that the old ways of governing would not meet the current needs of his subjects. Given this personal dilemma, Solomon requested a discerning heart, or wisdom, revealing a humble heart to the Lord.

What situation in your life right now makes you feel inadequate? What difference has God's wisdom made in how you have (or have not) dealt with that situation?

Ask a volunteer to read 1 Kings 3:10-13.

Why did Solomon's request please God? Can you think of another request that would have pleased God more than the desire for wisdom?

- Though Solomon could have asked for selfish favors such as wealth, long life, or revenge, he desired the ability to help others. Thus, in the first of four revelations to Solomon, God not only agreed to grant the request but made promises beyond what Solomon imagined.

- God was pleased that Solomon's request centered on the successful accomplishment of God's calling and not on worldly or self-centered desires. God listed three requests a self-focused king might have made in Solomon's situation: long life, riches, or the death of enemies. God promised to give Solomon a wise and understanding heart. He granted Solomon's request above and beyond what was asked, beginning with the kind of "heart" that would equip Solomon to rule effectively and justly over God's people. Because Solomon asked for things on behalf of God's people (see 3:9), God gave the honor and prestige of a worthy monarch.

What does God's willingness to give Solomon more than he asked for reveal about His nature? How have you witnessed God's generosity in your own life?

- God's willingness to give Solomon more than he requested demonstrates the generous and benevolent nature of God. He is a good God who loves to bless His people.

APPLY THE TEXT

Evaluate your priorities in light of Solomon's. In what ways do you value living with godly wisdom more than pursuing personal wealth or achievements?

What are some blessings that might accompany God-given wisdom, and how might you use such blessings in God's service?

SESSION 4 | LEADER GUIDE

FOCUS ATTENTION

Have you ever felt the need to make a clean break with your past? Explain.

EXPLORE THE TEXT

Ask a volunteer to read 2 Chronicles 14:1-5.

What is the author's theological assessment of Asa's reign overall? How did Asa's faithfulness impact the everyday lives of the people?

- Broadly speaking, Asa was a theologically sound leader who acted in accordance with his beliefs. Asa destroyed the illegitimate cult objects—altars, high places, the standing stones representing Baal, and the Asherah poles, wooden poles representing the goddess Asherah. As a result, the people experienced a significant degree of peace and prosperity.

Note the phrase "seek the Lord" in verse 4. What does it look like at a very practical level for people, both individually and corporately, to seek the Lord? What is the effect on both?

- For those in Asa's day, the phrase "seek the Lord" described how one was to respond to God, and thus defined one who was a member of the believing community. It involved more than a specific act of seeking God's help and guidance but stood for one's whole duty toward God. In other words, it is knowing God and being wholeheartedly devoted to Him. In Asa's time, this meant in part repentance from idol worship and the destruction of all that might have been a representation of that worship.

What forms of idol worship are prevalent in our culture today? What is appealing about them? What specific dangers to they pose to Christians?

- At its root meaning, idolatry is the worship of created things in place of the worship of Creator God. We live in an age of distraction. We are pulled in many different directions by technology, social media, friends, work, and hobbies. While none of these things are by definition "distractions," they can easily distract us from what is most important. God created us to love, worship, and enjoy Him. When we elevate anything to the place of God, that thing becomes an idol.

Why do you think we so easily fall into the trap of giving our hearts to idols? What are some of the excuses we use when rationalizing our emotional connection to idols?

- The idols of our current context may not literally be materials crafted into the form of a god, as some were in ancient times, but it is no less dangerous for us to give our affection and attention to lesser things in a way that borders on worship. We can identify these things that threaten to steal our worship by evaluating the things we give most time and attention to on a regular basis. What would observation of our daily routines lead one to believe is most important to us? Though it is foolish for us to worship these things, it does not mean we are any less prone to do so.

- Nothing outside of God can truly satisfy our souls. We are tempted to believe that lesser things will bring lasting satisfaction or enjoyment, even though experience tells us otherwise. Only through the person and work of Jesus Christ can we find true fulfillment and satisfaction. All other objects of worship will ultimately fail us.

Asa was said to have removed the high places from all the cities of Judah. Why is it important to be thorough when we begin to remove things that distract us from worshiping the true and living God?

- To leave one city's false places of worship untouched would invite disaster, because false worship could remain alive there and spread to other cities.

- It is important for us to obey God in our personal lives and to remove things that displease Him and could lead us astray. If we are not thorough, we invite sin to gain a toehold in our lives, something we are cautioned not to do in Ephesians 4.

Apply The Text

In what ways have you allowed your family background to keep you from serving the Lord? Based on Asa's example, is there any reason you could not make a break with the past and choose to begin serving the Lord today? Explain.

At its root meaning, idolatry is the worship of created things in place of the worship of Creator God. What created things are most tempting for you to worship or idolize: Money? Pleasure? Food? Toys? Work? Yourself? Why are you tempted by those things?

What does a life that truly has God in the primary place of worship look like? What are some of the key characteristics of this lifestyle?

SESSION 5 | LEADER GUIDE

FOCUS ATTENTION

If someone or something seemed determined to harm you or someone you love, to whom or what would you turn for help? Why?

EXPLORE THE TEXT

Ask a volunteer to read 2 Kings 18:28-32.

Suppose you were a Hebrew standing on the wall. How would you feel after hearing Rabshakeh's words?

- A Hebrew hearing these words probably felt terror as he thought about being conquered, deported, or killed by a foreign power. A Hebrew standing on Jerusalem's wall might also have felt abandoned by God, wondering why He was allowing a pagan nation to threaten His people in their capital.

- More positively, a Hebrew who heard the words of Rabshakeh might have felt a sense of excitement and daring, knowing that Israel's God was mighty and powerful, fully able to defend Jerusalem and all the people in it. Much like David felt when the Israelites were threatened by Goliath, Hezekiah had full confidence in God to bring victory in battle.

What "Rabshakeh" have you encountered in your life, someone who has tried to discourage you and tempt you to give up your trust in the Lord to rescue you? How do you respond to this type of objector?

- We have to make peace with those who don't support our beliefs and who try to discourage us. Follow what you know to be true and do not let anyone come in the way. Whether people support you or not, you don't want to look back in regret one day because you missed what God had for you.

Ask a volunteer to read 2 Kings 19:1-7.

What was Hezekiah's first response when he heard what Rabshakeh had said (vv. 1-2)? What did this response say about his character and relationship with the Lord?

- Hezekiah's first response was to repent, which was demonstrated by covering himself with sackcloth after tearing his clothes.

- Hezekiah's actions demonstrated that he was not too proud to humble himself before the Lord and in front of his people.

Ask a volunteer to read 2 Kings 19:14-19.

What did Hezekiah do with the threatening letter from Sennacherib? Why did he do this?

- Hezekiah read the letter, spread the letter out before the Lord in the temple, and then prayed to the God of heaven. Hezekiah placed the letter on the floor and covered the threat in prayer.

When have you figuratively or literally "spread . . . out before the Lord" something that was threatening you? What happened? How did this help?

- God will use our difficulties to our benefit (see Rom. 5:3-4). Our "worries" are an opportunity to trust the Lord for what we don't understand (see Prov. 3:5-6).

How did Hezekiah begin his prayer? Do you think this is important? Why or why not?

- Hezekiah began his prayer by stating that he was praying to the Lord of heaven, the One enthroned above the cherubim. He then praised God for making heaven and earth.

- Praising God is important so that you don't rush straight into a prayer of petition, but instead spend time focusing on the power, majesty, and wonder of who God is.

What reason did Hezekiah give for God to save His people? How should this impact your own prayers?

- Hezekiah prayed for God to save his people in order for the fame of the Lord to spread to other peoples on earth. Hezekiah wanted others to know that there is only one true God who is worthy of honor and glory.

APPLY THE TEXT

What is one situation in your life that has seemed so hopeless that you have stopped praying about it?

What are some specific ways the story of Hezekiah should influence your prayer life?

How can our group support you in prayer this week?

SESSION 6 | LEADER GUIDE

FOCUS ATTENTION

What kind of spiritual legacy did you grow up in? How did it affect your faith?

- People can positively influence others in their family to follow Christ by demonstrating faith in God, by leading in their church, through the example of their prayer and devotional life, and by speaking words of truth from Scripture.

- The generational influence is often seen in family members decades later as future generations choose to follow Christ themselves, living for God and serving Him in their churches, families, and communities.

EXPLORE THE TEXT

Ask a volunteer to read 2 Kings 21:19-24.

What characterized the reign of Amon, Josiah's father?

- Amon walked in the old idolatrous ways of his father Manasseh, sacrificing to the carved images in the land. He did not follow in Manasseh's call to serve the Lord of Israel only. Instead, he walked in pride and did much evil in the sight of the Lord, multiplying his sin and guilt. His palace servants conspired to kill him, and Amon's two-year reign ended at their hands. The people of the land executed those responsible for Amon's death and placed Josiah as king over Judah.

What might it have been like to grow up as a young boy under such a father? How might Amon's beliefs and choices have impacted young Josiah?

Ask a volunteer to read 2 Kings 22:1-7.

It is uncommon for the names of mothers to be mentioned when a kingly lineage is shared. Why might the author have put Josiah's mother's name in his story?

- One probable reason for mentioning Josiah's mother would be to at least subtly imply that many of the positive traits the reader would see in Josiah were at least partially due to her influence.

Josiah was blessed with the companionship of those who wanted what was right. They were loyal to Josiah and doubtless had an impact for godliness in the young child's life. What kind of influence do you think these men had on the young King Josiah?

- These men likely helped Josiah grow in his appreciation and reverence for God's Word. Josiah most likely learned excellent ethics from them. He saw their love for God and desire to do the right thing.

What benefits might have been associated with beginning religious reforms in the temple, as opposed to all the other places reform was needed in the land?

- Human beings are never more than who or what we worship. By beginning in the temple with his religious reforms, Josiah struck at the very heart of everyone's problem. By positioning them to worship God rightly, God would begin to do a work in the people's hearts.

Ask a volunteer to read 2 Kings 22:8-13.

Why did Josiah respond so strongly to what he read in the newly found Book of the Law? Was his reaction justified? Explain.

- Scripture greatly influenced Josiah's actions. Moses' writings were not obeyed through the centuries, but Josiah's personal commitment grew when he determined that God spoke to Moses and made a covenant with Israel. Josiah acted with the confidence that he was doing God's will, based on God's Word, in service to God's people. Josiah tore his garment when he heard God's Law, and sought a prophetic word to interpret the ramifications of his and the people's disobedience. He admitted the nation's sin, feared its results, and hoped it was not too late to change. He seemed to reason that God could act mercifully toward an undeserving people.

APPLY THE TEXT

What are some of the marks of Josiah's faith that are most meaningful to you?

How could you be a bigger influence in the life of someone who is young in his or her faith?

Who has had the most positive influence on your spiritual life so far? Call or write this person a note to show appreciation for his or her influence on you.

"Lord, there is no one besides you to help the mighty and those without strength. Help us, Lord our God, for we depend on you, and in your name we have come against this large army. Lord, you are our God. Do not let a mere mortal hinder you."

2 CHRONICLES 14:11

Whether you're a new Christian or you have believed in Jesus for several years, the people of the Bible have so much wisdom to offer. For that reason, we have created additional resources for churches that want to maximize the reach and impact of the *Characters* studies.

Complete Series Leader Pack

Want to take your group through the whole *Explore the Bible: Characters* series? You'll want a *Complete Series Leader Pack*. This *Pack* includes *Leader Kits* from Volume 1 - Volume 7. It allows you to take your group from The Patriarchs all the way to The Early Church Leaders.

$179.99

Video Bundle for Groups

All video sessions are available to purchase as a downloadable bundle.

$60.00

eBooks

A digital version of the *Bible Study Book* is also available for those who prefer studying with a phone or tablet. Some churches also find eBooks easier to distribute to study participants.

Starter Packs

You can save money and time by purchasing starter packs for your group or church. Every *Church Starter Pack* includes a digital *Church Launch Kit* and access to a digital version of the *Leader Kit* videos.

$99.99 | **Single Group Starter Pack**
(10 *Bible Study Books*, 1 *Leader Kit*)

$449.99 | **Small Church Starter Pack**
(50 *Bible Study Books*, 5 *Leader Kit* DVDs, and access to video downloads)

$799.99 | **Medium Church Starter Pack**
(100 *Bible Study Books*, 10 *Leader Kit* DVDs, and access to video downloads)

$3495.99 | **Large Church Starter Pack**
(500 *Bible Study Books*, 50 *Leader Kit* DVDs, and access to video downloads)

LifeWay.com/characters
Order online or call 800.458.2772.

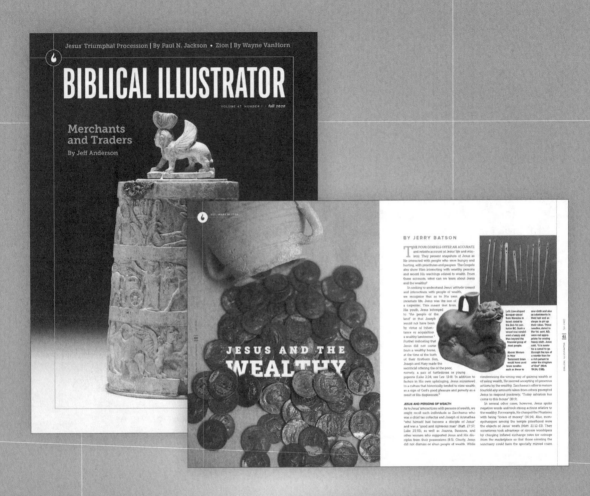

WANT TO KNOW EVEN MORE ABOUT BIBLICAL CHARACTERS?

The *Explore the Bible: Characters* series features information from the pages of *Biblical Illustrator*. And there are more insights on the way. Every quarter, you'll find remarkable content that will greatly enhance your study of the Bible:

- Fascinating photographs, illustrations, maps, and archaeological finds
- Informative articles on biblical lands, people, history, and customs
- Insights about how people lived, learned, and worshiped in biblical times

Order at lifeway.com/biblicalillustrator or call 800.458.2772.

Continue Your
Exploration

------------------------ VOLUME 4 ------------------------
THE PROPHETS

Studying the characters of the Bible helps us understand how God works in the world, loves His people, and moves through His people to accomplish His plans. The next volume of *Explore the Bible: Characters* focuses on Elijah, Jonah, Isaiah, Jeremiah, Ezekiel, and Malachi. Taking a closer look at these important prophets is an ideal way to wrap up our study of the Old Testament.

Bible Study Book   005823506   **$9.99**

EXPLORE YOUR OPTIONS

X EXPLORE THE BIBLE.

EXPLORE THE BIBLE

If you want to understand the Bible in its historical, cultural, and biblical context, few resources offer the thoroughness of the Explore the Bible ongoing quarterly curriculum. Over the course of nine years, you can study the whole truth, book by book, in a way that's practical, sustainable, and age appropriate for your entire church.

6- TO 8-WEEK STUDIES

If you're looking for short-term resources that are more small-group friendly, visit the LifeWay website to see Bible studies from a variety of noteworthy authors, including Ravi Zacharias, J.D. Greear, Matt Chandler, David Platt, Tony Evans, and many more.

Prices and availability subject to change without notice.